WHITBY TRAVEL GUIDE 2025

Discover Historic Landmarks, Coastal Adventures, and Local Delights in a Charming Seaside Town

Teresa Gilliam

Copyright © 2024 Teresa Gilliam All rights reserved.

No part of this book may be reproduced, stored in a retrieval system, or transmitted in any form or by any means, whether electronic, mechanical, photocopying, recording, scanning, or otherwise, without the publisher's prior written consent.

The work included herein is the sole property of the author and may not be reproduced or copied in any manner without the author's written consent. All information is provided "as is," without warranty of any kind, and liability is expressly disclaimed. The publisher and author expressly disclaim any duty for any loss, risk, or harm purportedly resulting from the use, application, or interpretation of the content contained herein.

MAP OF WHITBY

USE THE CODE TO SCAN FOR THE MAP

4 *WHITBY TRAVEL GUIDE 2024-2025*

TABLE OF CONTENTS

MAP OF WHITBY 3

INTRODUCTION TO WHITBY 9

    QUICK FACTS AND HISTORY 11

    HOW TO GET THERE 13

CHAPTER 1 15

    WHERE TO STAY 15

    TOP HOTELS AND GUESTHOUSES 15

    BUDGET ACCOMMODATIONS 19

    FAMILY-FRIENDLY STAYS 22

    UNIQUE LODGING EXPERIENCES 27

CHAPTER 2 31

    EXPLORING WHITBY 31

    MUST-SEE ATTRACTIONS 31

    HIDDEN GEMS AND LOCAL SECRETS 33

    WHITBY ABBEY AND ITS LEGACY 37

    HISTORIC SITES AND MUSEUMS 39

CHAPTER 3 42

    OUTDOOR ACTIVITIES 42

    BEST BEACHES AND COASTAL WALKS 42

5 *WHITBY TRAVEL GUIDE 2024-2025*

HIKING TRAILS AND NATURE RESERVES 45

WATER SPORTS AND FISHING 48

WILDLIFE WATCHING 51

CHAPTER 4 54

CULTURAL EXPERIENCES... 54

WHITBY FOLK WEEK... 54

LOCAL ART GALLERIES AND WORKSHOPS 56

LITERARY CONNECTIONS: BRAM STOKER AND DRACULA 58

MUSIC AND THEATRE VENUES 60

CHAPTER 5 63

DINING IN WHITBY 63

TOP RESTAURANTS AND CAFES 63

SEAFOOD SPECIALTIES 68

PUBS AND BREWERIES 70

VEGAN AND VEGETARIAN OPTIONS 73

CHAPTER 6 77

SHOPPING AND SOUVENIRS 77

LOCAL MARKETS AND SHOPS 77

ARTISANAL CRAFTS AND GIFTS 79

WHITBY JET JEWELRY 82

BOOKSTORES AND ANTIQUES 85

CHAPTER 7 88

FAMILY FUN 88

KID-FRIENDLY ATTRACTIONS 88

FAMILY ACTIVITIES AND EVENTS 91

PARKS AND PLAYGROUNDS 93

CHAPTER 8 95

EVENTS AND FESTIVALS 95

ANNUAL EVENTS CALENDAR 95

WHITBY GOTH WEEKEND 97

MARITIME FESTIVALS 99

FOOD AND DRINK FESTIVALS 102

CHAPTER 9 104

DAY TRIPS AND EXCURSIONS 104

NEARBY COASTAL VILLAGES 104

NORTH YORK MOORS NATIONAL PARK 107

HISTORIC SITES IN THE REGION 109

SCENIC TRAIN RIDES 112

CHAPTER 10 114

7 WHITBY TRAVEL GUIDE 2024-2025

PRACTICAL INFORMATION 114

TRANSPORTATION AND GETTING AROUND............... 114

HEALTH AND SAFETY TIPS... 117

ACCESSIBILITY INFORMATION 119

LOCAL ETIQUETTE AND CUSTOMS................................ 121

CHAPTER 11 123

SUSTAINABLE TRAVEL 123

ECO-FRIENDLY ACCOMMODATION 123

GREEN ACTIVITIES AND TOURS 125

SUPPORTING LOCAL BUSINESSES 128

TIPS FOR REDUCING YOUR CARBON FOOTPRINT 130

CONCLUSION 133

INTRODUCTION TO WHITBY

Step into the timeless charm of Whitby, where the whispers of history resonate down cobblestone streets and the salty breeze from the North Sea conveys legends of old. As an eager explorer of the world's hidden gems, I've journeyed through many corners of this planet, although few places have fascinated me quite like Whitby. Nestled on the rugged Yorkshire coastline, this little coastal town is not simply a destination; it's a journey through centuries of nautical legend, Gothic romance, and natural beauty.

Imagine meandering along the cliffside trails, where the haunting silhouette of Whitby Abbey stands guard against the sky, its ancient stones bearing witness to a past steeped in folklore. Below, the harbor bustles with life, fishermen's tales blending with the laughter of visitors eating fresh fish and chips. From the little alleyways dotted with centuries-old cottages to the huge lengths of sandy beaches that call with every tide, Whitby unfolds like a narrative waiting to be explored.

In producing this guidebook, I aim to unravel the layers of Whitby's fascination, offering you not just practical suggestions but a narrative that enables you to immerse yourself totally in its mystique. Whether you're tracing the footsteps of Captain Cook, discovering the exquisite shops of Church Street, or simply finding peace in the beat of the waves, Whitby guarantees an experience that remains long after you've left its beaches.

Join me on this tour through twisting alleys and panoramic overlooks, where every bend unveils a new chapter in Whitby's tale. Let this guide be your companion as you negotiate the cobblestones and explore the hidden gems that make Whitby a treasure trove for visitors and dreamers alike.

Welcome to Whitby where history meets the horizon, and every visit becomes a voyage of discovery.

QUICK FACTS AND HISTORY

Whitby is a charming coastal town in North Yorkshire, England, known for its rich past and striking scenery. This small town has captured the hearts of many with its unique blend of historical importance and natural beauty.

Quick Facts:

Location: North Yorkshire, England

Population: Approximately 13,000

Famous for: Whitby Abbey, Captain Cook Memorial Museum, Dracula links

Main industries: Tourism, fishing, and jet jewelry

History: Whitby's story goes back to the 7th century when the famous Whitby Abbey was founded by St. Hilda in 657 AD. The Abbey quickly became a center of learning and religion, playing a pivotal part in the Synod of Whitby in 664 AD, which helped to determine the future of the English church.

The town's maritime history flourished in the 18th century, largely due to Captain James Cook, the famous explorer who began his naval career in Whitby. The Captain Cook Memorial Museum in Whitby offers a deep dive into his life and travels.

Whitby's unique link to Bram Stoker's Dracula has also made it a popular destination for literary enthusiasts. Stoker was inspired by the town's dramatic cliffs and eerie abbey ruins when writing his famous book. Today, visitors can experience the Dracula Experience, a walk-through attraction that brings the novel to life.

The town's economy previously revolved around the fishing industry, and Whitby's harbor is still active with fishing boats bringing in daily catches. Another major industry is jet jewelry. Whitby jet, a fossilized wood, has been used since the Victorian era to make exquisite jewelry pieces.

Whitby is not only rich in history but also offers a warm community and vibrant cultural scene. Festivals such as the Whitby Goth Weekend and the Whitby Folk Week celebrate the town's diverse history and attract tourists from all over the world.

HOW TO GET THERE

By Car

Driving to Whitby offers the flexibility to explore the nearby countryside at your own pace. From London, take the M1 motorway northbound, then turn onto the A1(M). Continue until you reach the A19, which will lead you straight to Whitby. If you're coming from the north, follow the A1(M) southbound, then take the A171 towards Whitby. The scenic route through the North York Moors National Park offers breathtaking views and is well worth the extra time.

By Train

Traveling by train is a convenient and scenic choice. From London King's Cross, take a direct train to York, which usually takes about two hours. From York, transfer to a Northern Rail train that will take you to Middlesbrough. At Middlesbrough, take another Northern Rail train to Whitby. The entire trip offers a relaxing and picturesque view of the English countryside and takes approximately four hours.

By Bus

If you prefer traveling by bus, several services connect major towns to Whitby. From London, you can take a National Express coach to Middlesbrough, where you can switch to a local bus service that will take you to Whitby. Alternatively, from Leeds or York, you can take a Coastliner bus, which offers direct routes to Whitby, allowing you to enjoy the scenic trip through the Yorkshire landscape.

By Air

For foreign visitors, the nearest major airport is Newcastle Foreign Airport, which is about 75 miles from Whitby. From the airport, you can take a train or bus to Whitby. Alternatively, Leeds Bradford Airport is another option, located roughly 80 miles from Whitby. Both airports offer different transportation options, including car rentals, trains, and buses.

By Ferry

If you're coming from Europe, you can take a ferry to Hull, which is about a two-hour drive from Whitby. P&O Ferries runs regular services from Rotterdam and Zeebrugge to Hull. From Hull, you can drive, take a train, or hop on a bus to reach Whitby. The ferry route gives a unique and enjoyable travel experience, especially during the warmer months.

CHAPTER 1

WHERE TO STAY

TOP HOTELS AND GUESTHOUSES

1. The White Horse & Griffin

Location: 87 Church Street, Whitby YO22 4BH, UK

Description: This historic hotel, dating back to 1681, is a favorite among visitors. It features charming rooms with modern amenities, and its on-site restaurant is known for delicious meals. Located in the heart of Whitby, it's a great base for exploring the town.

Phone: +44 1947 825026

Price: $100-$150 per night

2. The Marine Hotel

Location: 13 Marine Parade, Whitby YO21 3PR, UK

Description: Situated along the harbor, The Marine Hotel provides beautiful sea views. The rooms are stylish and comfortable, with some featuring balconies. Guests often praise the friendly service and excellent breakfast.

Phone: +44 1947 605022

Price: $120-$180 per night

3. The Resolution Hotel

Location: 1 Skinner Street, Whitby YO21 3AH, UK

Description: Known for its central location, The Resolution Hotel offers easy access to Whitby's attractions. The rooms are cozy and well-equipped, and the hotel features a lively bar and restaurant. It's ideal for those who want to be close to the action.

Phone: +44 1947 602085

Price: $80-$130 per night

4. La Rosa Hotel

Location: 5 East Terrace, Whitby YO21 3HB, UK

Description: La Rosa Hotel is famous for its quirky, themed rooms, each with a unique character. This boutique hotel offers a fun and different experience, perfect for those looking for something out of the ordinary. The rooms provide a wonderful outlook.

Phone: +44 1947 606981

Price: $130-$200 per night

5. The Waverley Guest House

Location: 17 Crescent Avenue, Whitby YO21 3ED, UK

Description: This family-run guesthouse is known for its warm hospitality. The Waverley offers comfortable rooms and a hearty breakfast to start your day. It's located in a quiet area but still close to Whitby's main attractions.

Phone: +44 1947 604389

Price: $70-$100 per night

6. Rylstone Mere

Location: 30 Bagdale, Whitby YO21 1QL, UK

Description: Rylstone Mere is a charming bed and breakfast that offers a peaceful retreat. The rooms are clean and spacious, and the hosts are known for their helpfulness. It's a great option for anyone who likes a more laid-back vibe.

Phone: +44 1947 602341

Price: $90-$120 per night

7. Pannett House

Location: 14 Normanby Terrace, Whitby YO21 1ET, UK

Description: Pannett House combines Victorian charm with modern comfort. The guesthouse features elegantly decorated rooms and a lovely garden where guests can unwind. It's close to Pannett Park and a short walk from the harbor.

Phone: +44 1947 602907

Price: $85-$110 per night

8. The Belfry Whitby

Location: 2 Church Square, Whitby YO21 3EG, UK

Description: Located in a converted chapel, The Belfry offers a unique stay with beautifully designed rooms. The guesthouse is praised for its welcoming atmosphere and delicious breakfasts. It's conveniently situated near the town center.

Phone: +44 1947 820228

Price: $100-$140 per night

9. The Sands - Sea Front Apartments

Location: 2-4 North Terrace, Whitby YO21 3JR, UK

Description: For those seeking more space, The Sands offers luxurious apartments with stunning sea views. Each unit is fully equipped with modern conveniences, making it ideal for families or longer stays.

Phone: +44 1947 824525

Price: $150-$250 per night

10. Ellie's Guest House

Location: 4 Langdale Terrace, Whitby YO21 1RB, UK

Description: This cozy guesthouse is known for its friendly service and comfortable rooms. Ellie's Guest House provides a welcoming atmosphere, and the hosts are always ready to give tips on local attractions.

Phone: +44 1947 604315

Price: $60-$90 per night

BUDGET ACCOMMODATIONS

1. YHA Whitby

Location: Abbey House, East Cliff, Whitby, YO22 4JT

Phone: +44 345 371 9655

Price: Starting at $30 per night

Description: Located right next to the iconic Whitby Abbey, YHA Whitby provides clean and comfortable dormitory-style rooms and private rooms. The hostel has a friendly atmosphere, a self-catering kitchen, and an on-site café. It's perfect for travelers who want an affordable place to stay with a great view.

2. Pannett House Bed and Breakfast

Location: 14 Normanby Terrace, Whitby, YO21 3ES

Phone: +44 194 760 5102

Price: Starting at $50 per night

Description: Pannett House offers cozy rooms with traditional décor and modern amenities. The B&B serves a delicious breakfast each morning, included in the room rate. It's conveniently located within walking distance of Whitby's main attractions, making it a great option for budget-conscious travelers.

3. The Whitby Way

Location: 37 Bagdale, Whitby, YO21 1QL

Phone: +44 194 760 6698

Price: Starting at $45 per night

Description: This guesthouse provides comfortable rooms at affordable rates. The Whitby Way is known for its warm hospitality and clean, well-maintained rooms. Guests can enjoy a complimentary breakfast and easy access to the town center.

4. The Shepherd's Purse

Location: 95 Church Street, Whitby, YO22 4BH

Phone: +44 194 760 2471

Price: Starting at $55 per night

Description: The Shepherd's Purse offers unique, individually decorated rooms in a charming setting. This family-run establishment prides itself on offering a welcoming atmosphere and personalized service. It's located in the heart of Whitby's old town, close to many attractions and dining options.

5. Sanders Yard

Location: 95 Church Street, Whitby, YO22 4BH

Phone: +44 194 760 2231

Price: Starting at $60 per night

Description: Sanders Yard provides comfortable accommodations with a touch of rustic charm. The rooms are tastefully decorated, and the café serves delicious homemade meals and treats. It's an ideal spot for those looking to explore Whitby on foot.

Tips for Budget Travelers

1. Book in Advance: Accommodations in Whitby can fill up quickly, especially during peak seasons. You can get the best deals if you make your reservation in advance.

2. Travel Off-Season: Visiting Whitby during the off-peak season can save you money on both accommodations and attractions.

3. Utilize Public Transportation: Whitby is well-connected by public transportation. Using buses and trains can be more cost-effective than renting a car.

4. Self-Catering Options: Consider staying in places with self-catering facilities to save on dining costs.

5. Explore Free Attractions: Whitby offers many free attractions, such as its beautiful beaches and scenic walking trails.

FAMILY-FRIENDLY STAYS

1. The White Horse & Griffin

Location: 87 Church Street, Whitby, YO22 4BH

Description: The White Horse & Griffin is a charming hotel located in the heart of Whitby. Its cozy family rooms are perfect for a relaxing stay. The on-site restaurant serves delicious meals suitable for all ages, and the hotel's central location makes it easy to explore nearby attractions.

Tips: Request a room with a view of the harbor for a pleasant experience.

Phone Number: +44 1947 604857

Prices: Rooms start at $120 per night.

2. Raithwaite Sandsend

Location: Sandsend Road, Whitby, YO21 3ST

Description: Raithwaite Sandsend is a luxurious family-friendly resort set on a stunning estate. The resort offers spacious family suites, an indoor pool, and extensive gardens. It is a short walk from the beach, making it ideal for families who enjoy seaside activities.

Tips: Take advantage of the complimentary shuttle service to Whitby town center.

Phone Number: +44 1947 661661

Prices: Family rooms start at $200 per night.

3. The Dolphin Hotel

Location: Bridge Street, Whitby, YO22 4BG

Description: The Dolphin Hotel is a traditional inn located near Whitby's famous swing bridge. It offers family-friendly accommodations with modern amenities. The hotel has a welcoming atmosphere and a menu that caters to children's tastes.

Tips: Book a room overlooking the River Esk for a peaceful stay.

Phone Number: +44 1947 821455

Prices: Rooms start at $110 per night.

4. The Seacliffe Hotel

Location: 12 North Promenade, Whitby, YO21 3JX

Description: The Seacliffe Hotel is ideally situated on Whitby's West Cliff, offering breathtaking sea views. Family rooms are available, and the hotel's location provides easy access to the beach and local attractions. The hotel also has a spacious garden for children to play in.

Tips: Enjoy a family walk along the coastal path for some fresh air and exercise.

Phone Number: +44 1947 602461

Prices: Family rooms start at $130 per night.

5. The Waverley Guest House

Location: 17 Crescent Avenue, Whitby, YO21 3ED

Description: The Waverley Guest House is a family-run establishment that offers a warm and friendly atmosphere. The guest house has comfortable family rooms and is located just a short walk from the beach and Whitby's main attractions.

Tips: Take advantage of the homemade breakfast to start your day off right.

Phone Number: +44 1947 603644

Prices: Rooms start at $100 per night.

6. The Saxonville Hotel

Location: Ladysmith Avenue, Whitby, YO21 3HX

Description: The Saxonville Hotel is a Victorian-style hotel located on the West Cliff. It offers family rooms with elegant decor and modern amenities. The hotel's restaurant serves delicious meals, and the location is perfect for exploring Whitby's historic sites.

Tips: Visit Pannett Park nearby for a family picnic.

Phone Number: +44 1947 602631

Prices: Family rooms start at $140 per night.

7. Whitby Holiday Park

Location: Saltwick Bay, Whitby, YO22 4JX

Description: Whitby Holiday Park offers a range of family-friendly accommodations, including caravans and lodges. The park has excellent facilities, such as a playground, a shop, and a café. Its location near Saltwick Bay makes it ideal for beach outings and fossil hunting.

Tips: Participate in the organized family activities for added fun.

Phone Number: +44 1947 602664

Prices: Lodges start at $90 per night.

8. The Captain Cook Inn

Location: 60 Staithes Lane, Staithes, Whitby, TS13 5AD

Description: The Captain Cook Inn is a family-friendly pub with rooms located in the charming village of Staithes, near Whitby. The inn offers comfortable family rooms and a restaurant with a kid-friendly menu. The nearby beach and picturesque village are great for exploring.

Tips: Explore the nearby Captain Cook & Staithes Heritage Centre for an educational experience.

Phone Number: +44 1947 840200

Prices: Rooms start at $105 per night.

9. Discovery Accommodation

Location: 11 Silver Street, Whitby, YO21 3BX

Description: Discovery Accommodation offers a variety of family-friendly apartments and cottages in central Whitby. Each unit is equipped with a kitchen, making it easy to prepare meals for the family. The accommodations are close to Whitby's main attractions and the beach.

Tips: Choose an apartment with a balcony for outdoor dining.

Phone Number: +44 1947 821127

Prices: Apartments start at $120 per night.

10. Sanders Yard

Location: 95 Church Street, Whitby, YO22 4BH

Description: Sanders Yard provides cozy family rooms and cottages in the heart of Whitby's old town. The accommodations have a unique charm, with modern amenities ensuring a comfortable stay. The on-site café serves breakfast and light meals, perfect for families.

Tips: Explore the nearby Whitby Abbey for a bit of history and great views.

Phone Number: +44 1947 825010

Prices: Rooms start at $115 per night.

UNIQUE LODGING EXPERIENCES

1. La Rosa Hotel

Location: 5 East Terrace, Whitby, YO21 3HB

Phone Number: +44 1947 606981

Price: From £100 per night

Description: La Rosa Hotel is a quirky and artistic boutique hotel overlooking the sea. Each room is themed, drawing inspiration from Whitby's rich history and literary connections. Guests can enjoy Victorian-style décor, vintage furnishings, and stunning views of the coastline. The hotel offers a complimentary breakfast with locally sourced ingredients and a warm, welcoming atmosphere.

2. The Stables at Cross Butts

Location: Guisborough Road, Whitby, YO21 1TL

Phone Number: +44 1947 820986

Price: From £120 per night

Description: The Stables at Cross Butts offers a rustic countryside retreat with the convenience of being just a short drive from Whitby. This converted stable provides cozy and comfortable accommodations with modern amenities. The on-site restaurant serves hearty meals made from locally sourced produce, ensuring a true farm-to-table experience. Guests can also explore the beautiful surrounding gardens and enjoy the peaceful rural setting.

3. Dillons of Whitby

Location: 14 Chubb Hill Road, Whitby, YO21 1JU

Phone Number: +44 1947 600290

Price: From £140 per night

Description: Dillons of Whitby is a luxurious bed and breakfast that combines elegance with comfort. The property features individually styled rooms with high-quality furnishings and modern facilities. Guests can enjoy a delicious breakfast made with local ingredients, as well as personalized service that makes you feel at home. The central location allows easy access to Whitby's attractions, including the harbor and the historic Whitby Abbey.

4. The Shepherd's Purse

Location: 95 Church Street, Whitby, YO22 4BH

Phone Number: +44 1947 820228

Price: From £90 per night

Description: The Shepherd's Purse is a charming guesthouse located in the heart of Whitby's old town. This quaint accommodation offers beautifully decorated rooms, each with its unique style and character. The peaceful garden provides a perfect spot for relaxation. The friendly hosts are always ready to offer tips on the best local spots to visit. It's an ideal choice for those looking to experience Whitby's vibrant culture and history.

5. Raithwaite Estate

Location: Sandsend Road, Whitby, YO21 3ST

Phone Number: +44 1947 661661

Price: From £200 per night

Description: Raithwaite Estate offers a luxurious escape with its expansive grounds and high-end amenities. The estate features a range of accommodations, including elegant rooms, suites, and private cottages. Guests can enjoy the on-site spa, indoor pool, and fine dining restaurant. The beautifully landscaped gardens and proximity to Sandsend Beach make it a perfect getaway for those seeking both relaxation and adventure.

CHAPTER 2

EXPLORING WHITBY

MUST-SEE ATTRACTIONS

One of the most recognizable sites in the town is Whitby Abbey. This abandoned Gothic abbey is steeped in history and is perched on a cliff overlooking the North Sea. With breathtaking views of the town and ocean, the abbey was built in the seventh century. The visitor center offers intriguing insights into the history of the abbey, so it's worth spending the time to look around. Recall to ascend the 199 steps that go to the abbey for a quick workout and fantastic picture ops.

Visit the Captain Cook Memorial Museum to get a flavor of Whitby's maritime history. The legendary explorer Captain James Cook formerly resided in the 17th-century home that now serves as the museum. A look into Cook's adventurous life is offered by the museum's collection of items and displays relating to his expeditions. Families and history buffs will both enjoy this location.

Another gem is Whitby's port. It's a busy place with pleasure boats, fishing boats, and small stores. Enjoy the clean sea air and the passing boats as you stroll around the port. You can enjoy regional specialties, like Whitby's famous fish and chips, at any number of seafood restaurants and cafes. Fortune's Kippers is a family-run smokehouse that has been making mouthwatering smoked fish for more than 140 years. Don't miss it.

For a peaceful day by the sea, Whitby Beach is ideal. The long, sandy beach is perfect for a stroll or an enjoyable day spent with the family. You can lounge with a nice book, make sandcastles, or surf the waves. Being patrolled by lifeguards during the summer makes the beach a safe place to swim.

In the center of Whitby is a beautiful green area called Pannett Park. The Whitby Museum and Pannett Art Gallery are located in this exquisitely designed park. Fossils, jet jewelry, and local history exhibits are among the varied treasures in the museum's collection. Temporary exhibitions and artwork by regional artists are showcased at the art gallery. A picnic or a stroll amid the trees and flowers is a wonderful idea in the park itself.

Strolling along the Cleveland Way National Trail is a great way to take in Whitby's breathtaking natural surroundings. With its expansive stretches of walking trails along the shore, this walk provides amazing views of the sea and the rocks. The popular route that passes through charming villages and breathtaking scenery is the one that runs from Whitby to Robin Hood's Bay.

Take a Whitby ghost walk for a memorable and eerie experience. Along with sharing spooky stories of local legends and paranormal encounters, these guided tours take you through some of the town's most haunted locations. It gives your stay a little extra adventure and is an interesting opportunity to learn about Whitby's troubled past.

Because they can change, it's crucial to confirm the attraction opening hours and entry costs when making travel plans to Whitby. It's worthwhile to investigate the many locations that provide family tickets or discounts for elders and students. It's best to arrive early or take public transportation as parking can be scarce, particularly during the busiest travel times.

HIDDEN GEMS AND LOCAL SECRETS

Sandsend Beach

While Whitby Beach attracts many visitors, Sandsend Beach, just a short drive away, offers a quieter option. This stretch of sand is great for a peaceful stroll, collecting seashells, or enjoying a picnic. The village of Sandsend itself is quaint and picturesque, with charming houses and a couple of lovely cafes. For a relaxed day out, visit Sandsend and take in the serene coastal views.

Pannett Park

Located in the heart of Whitby, Pannett Park is a delightful green area often overlooked by tourists. The park features beautifully landscaped gardens, a playground, and the Whitby Museum, which houses interesting local artifacts. It's an ideal spot for a leisurely walk or a family trip. Don't miss the stunning views of the town and bay from the park's highest points.

The Old Smuggler's Tunnel

Whitby's past is rich with tales of smugglers and hidden tunnels. One such tunnel can be found near the Khyber Pass, going from the harbor area to the cliffs. Though it's no longer in use, exploring this historic cave gives a sense of the town's adventurous past. Be sure to bring a flashlight and wear sturdy shoes, as the ground can be uneven.

Whitby Brewery

Nestled beside the famous Whitby Abbey, the Whitby Brewery is a hidden gem for beer enthusiasts. This small, independent brewery makes a range of craft beers, each with its unique flavor. Take a walk to learn about the brewing process and enjoy a tasting session. The brewery's terrace offers spectacular views of the abbey and the nearby landscape.

Captain Cook Memorial Museum

While not exactly hidden, the Captain Cook Memorial Museum is often overshadowed by other sights. Located in the 17th-century house where Cook served his apprenticeship, the museum offers a fascinating look into the life and voyages of one of history's greatest explorers. The collection includes maps, letters, and artifacts from Cook's journeys, offering a deep dive into maritime history.

Fortune's Kippers

A visit to Whitby wouldn't be complete without trying its famous smoked kippers. Fortune's Kippers, a family-run business started in 1872, is tucked away on Henrietta Street. Their traditional smokehouse makes some of the best kippers in the country. Stop by to taste these delicious fish and learn about the age-old smoking process. Remember to take some home for a truly unique Whitby experience.

Falling Foss Tea Garden

Hidden in the woods near Sneaton Forest, Falling Foss Tea Garden is a magical spot to unwind. The tea garden is set beside a beautiful waterfall, providing a peaceful setting for a cup of tea and homemade scones. There are also several walking trails in the area, making it a great destination for nature lovers. The garden is seasonal, so check opening times before your visit.

Whitby Jet Workshops

Whitby is famous for its jet, a black gemstone made from fossilized wood. While many shops sell jet jewelry, visiting a workshop offers a more full experience. Several local artists have workshops where you can see the crafting process and even try your hand at making a piece of jet jewelry. These workshops provide a unique souvenir and a deeper respect for this local craft.

Hidden Alleyways and Yards

Whitby's narrow alleyways and secret yards are steeped in history and character. Exploring these lesser-known paths shows charming houses, secret gardens, and unique shops. Start your trip around Church Street and the East Side, where you'll find plenty of nooks and crannies to explore. Each turn offers a glimpse into Whitby's past and the everyday life of its people.

Tips for Exploring Whitby's Hidden Gems:

1. Wear comfortable walking shoes, as many hidden spots take a bit of a walk.

2. Bring a camera to record the beautiful and unexpected sights.

3. Visit local cafes and shops to support the community and get secret tips from residents.

4. Check the opening hours of sites and plan your visit accordingly.

5. Take your time and enjoy the slower pace of finding Whitby's secrets.

WHITBY ABBEY AND ITS LEGACY

Perched atop cliffs with a commanding view of the North Sea is Whitby Abbey, a truly amazing location. The town of Whitby in North Yorkshire, England, is famous for its striking ruins. St. Hilda founded the abbey in 657 AD, and it has a long and illustrious history spanning more than a thousand years, notable for its influence on literature and culture as well as its role in the spread of Christianity.

Visitors come from all over the world to see the abbey's stunning Gothic architecture, which features elaborate masonry and soaring arches. The magnificence of the monastery is apparent despite its state of ruin. Offering a broad perspective of Whitby and the coast, the site's views are stunning. Bram Stoker was one of the writers, poets, and artists who was influenced by the magnificent monastery. He used it as the backdrop for his well-known novel "Dracula."

The Synod of Whitby in 664 AD is one of the most important occasions in the abbey's history. This assembly was essential to figuring out how Easter was calculated and bringing the English Church's customs into line with those of Rome. This synod's decision had a long-term effect on the spread of Christianity in England.

Over the ages, Whitby Abbey encountered several difficulties, such as Viking attacks in the ninth century and Henry VIII's dissolution in the sixteenth century. The abbey's heritage persisted despite these difficulties. The ruins came to represent tenacity and served as a reminder of the rich history of the region.

The abbey is a well-liked tourist destination today, run by English Heritage. The visitor center features interactive exhibits and displays that let visitors explore the ruins and discover more about its history. To preserve the abbey's history for future generations, the site also organizes several year-round events, such as historical reenactments and educational courses.

HISTORIC SITES AND MUSEUMS

1. Whitby Abbey

Whitby Abbey, perched on a cliff overlooking the town, is one of the most iconic sites in Whitby. This stunning ruin goes back to the 7th century and has inspired writers like Bram Stoker, the author of "Dracula." The abbey offers stunning views of the town and the North Sea.

Location: Abbey Lane, Whitby, YO22 4JT

Description: The gothic ruins of Whitby Abbey are a sight to behold, giving insight into the region's religious history and architectural evolution.

Tips: Visit early in the morning or late afternoon to avoid crowds and capture the best photos.

Entry Fee: Adults £10, children £6, and family tickets £26.

2. Captain Cook Memorial Museum

This museum is dedicated to the life and travels of Captain James Cook, the famous British explorer. It is kept in the 17th-century house where Cook lodged as an apprentice.

Location: Grape Lane, Whitby, YO22 4BA

Description: The museum includes original letters, maps, and artifacts from Cook's voyages. Interactive displays and shows make it a fascinating visit for all ages.

Tips: Allow at least an hour to explore the museum fully and take advantage of the guided tours available.

Entry Fee: Adults £7, children £3, and family tickets £15.

3. Whitby Museum

Located in Pannett Park, Whitby Museum highlights the town's local history, geology, and maritime heritage. It's a treasure trove of interesting exhibits, including fossils, model ships, and a hand of glory.

Location: Pannett Park, Whitby, YO21 1RE

Description: This museum offers a complete view of Whitby's past, from its prehistoric fossils to its whaling industry. The extensive collection offers a unique glimpse into the town's evolution over the centuries.

Tips: Don't miss the collection of jet jewelry and the famous Hand of Glory display.

Entry Fee: Adults £5, children £3, and family tickets £12.

4. St. Mary's Church

St. Mary's Church, dating back to the 12th century, stands near Whitby Abbey and offers a peaceful retreat with amazing views of the harbor.

Location: Church Street, Whitby, YO22 4DN

Description: The church's unique interior, with its box pews and historic memorials, represents the town's rich heritage. It also serves as a resting place for many sailors and local people.

Tips: Climb the 199 steps going to the church for a panoramic view of Whitby and its surroundings.

Entry Fee: Free, but donations are welcomed.

5. The Endeavour Experience

Step aboard a full-scale model of Captain Cook's ship, the HM Bark Endeavour, and experience life at sea in the 18th century.

Location: Endeavour Wharf, Whitby, YO21 1DN

Description: This interactive attraction gives a hands-on experience, allowing guests to explore the ship's cabins, deck, and cargo hold while learning about Cook's voyages and maritime history.

Tips: Participate in the guided tours for a more in-depth understanding of the ship and its importance.

Entry Fee: Adults £6, children £4, and family tickets £14.

CHAPTER 3

OUTDOOR ACTIVITIES

BEST BEACHES AND COASTAL WALKS

Best Beaches in Whitby

1. Whitby Beach

Whitby Beach, located on the east coast, is a favorite spot for families and tourists alike. The beach is known for its golden sands, great for sunbathing, building sandcastles, or taking a leisurely walk along the shore. Whitby Beach is easily accessible from the town center, and parking is available close by. Dogs are allowed on parts of the beach, making it a great spot for a family day out. There are no entry fees, but you might need to pay for parking.

2. Sandsend Beach

A short drive north of Whitby, Sandsend Beach offers a quieter, more serene beach experience. The beach runs for miles, providing ample space for beachcombing and exploring rock pools. The village of Sandsend has lovely cafes and restaurants where you can enjoy a meal with a sea view. Parking is available close to the beach, and there are no entry fees. It's a great place for a peaceful retreat.

3. Robin Hood's Bay

Robin Hood's Bay, located about six miles south of Whitby, is a picturesque coastal village with a rich past. The beach here is great for fossil hunting and discovering tidal pools. The town itself is a maze of narrow streets and quaint cottages, making it a delightful place to wander. Parking is available at the top of the village, and a steep walk down goes to the beach. There are no entry fees, but be prepared for a workout on the way back up!

Coastal Walks in Whitby

1. Whitby to Sandsend Walk

This coastal walk is a favorite among locals and tourists. The path starts at Whitby Beach and tracks the coastline north to Sandsend. The walk offers amazing views of the North Sea and the rugged cliffs. It's a relatively easy walk, good for most fitness levels, and takes about 1.5 hours one way. Be sure to wear comfortable shoes and bring a camera to record the breathtaking scenery. There are no entry fees, and you can catch a bus back to Whitby if you prefer not to walk both ways.

2. Cleveland Way National Trail

The Cleveland Way is a long-distance footpath that runs 109 miles from Helmsley to Filey. The section from Whitby to Robin Hood's Bay is particularly scenic, giving dramatic views of the coastline and the North York Moors. This walk is more difficult due to its length and uneven terrain, but it's well worth the effort. The route is well-marked, and you can find plenty of places to rest along the way. There are no entry fees, but make sure to bring plenty of drinks and snacks.

3. Whitby Abbey and the 199 Steps

For a shorter but equally satisfying walk, head to Whitby Abbey. The walk starts at the bottom of the 199 Steps, a historic staircase that goes up to the Abbey. Along the way, you'll get panoramic views of the bay and town. At the top, discover the ruins of Whitby Abbey, a site steeped in history and legend. Entry to the Abbey itself needs a fee (approximately £10 for adults, with discounts for children and seniors), but the views from the steps are free.

Tips for Visiting Weather:

1. The weather in Whitby can be uncertain, so bring layers and be prepared for rain.

2. Footwear: Wear comfortable walking shoes, especially for coastal walks, as some roads can be uneven and slippery.

3. Facilities: Public restrooms are provided at most beaches and key points along the walks.

4. Dogs: Many beaches and walks are dog-friendly, but always check local laws.

HIKING TRAILS AND NATURE RESERVES

Whitby to Robin Hood's Bay

This classic coastal walk runs approximately 7 miles from Whitby to Robin Hood's Bay. The trail offers breathtaking sea views, dramatic cliffs, and charming coastal towns. Starting at Whitby Abbey, the path follows the Cleveland Way National Trail, offering a mix of rugged terrain and well-maintained paths. This hike is moderately challenging, making it ideal for most fitness levels.

The Cinder Track

The Cinder Track is a 21-mile path that runs from Whitby to Scarborough, following the old railway line. This trail is great for both walking and cycling, with a relatively flat and even surface. Along the way, travelers can enjoy the scenic scenery, cross viaducts, and explore small towns and villages. The track is a great option for families and those wanting a leisurely outdoor experience.

Falling Foss and May Beck

A shorter, yet equally captivating walk is the Falling Foss and May Beck trail. This 2.5-mile circular path takes visitors through enchanting woodland and along the peaceful May Beck stream. The highlight of the walk is Falling Foss, a 30-foot waterfall surrounded by lush greenery. There is a lovely tea garden near the waterfall where hikers can rest and enjoy refreshments.

Mulgrave Woods

Mulgrave Woods, located just a few miles from Whitby, offers a network of trails through old woodland. The paths meander through the forest, showing hidden streams, historic ruins, and a diverse range of flora and fauna. These trails are ideal for a tranquil walk, providing a serene break from the hustle and bustle of town life. The woods are privately owned, but access is usually allowed on Sundays.

North York Moors National Park

A visit to Whitby would not be complete without visiting the North York Moors National Park. The park boasts an extensive network of hiking trails, giving routes that range from easy strolls to challenging hikes. Popular walks include the Esk Valley Walk, which follows the River Esk, and the Lyke Wake Walk, a demanding 40-mile trek across the moors. The park's varied landscapes include heather-clad moorland, deep valleys, and ancient forests.

Saltwick Bay

For a seaside walk with a difference, head to Saltwick Bay. This area is known for its striking geological features, including sea stacks and fossil-rich rocks. The walk from Whitby to Saltwick Bay is around 2 miles and offers chances for fossil hunting, rock pooling, and exploring the dramatic coastline. It's a relatively easy walk, making it good for families and casual hikers.

Sandsend to Runswick Bay

Another beautiful coastal hike is the path from Sandsend to Runswick Bay. This 6-mile trail follows the Cleveland Way and offers amazing views of the North Sea. Hikers will pass through peaceful beaches, cliff tops, and quaint fishing towns. The trail is moderately challenging, with some steep parts, but the breathtaking views make it well worth the effort.

Sneaton Forest

Sneaton Forest, located a short drive from Whitby, is a secret gem for nature lovers. The forest features a variety of trails that wind through thick woodland, open glades, and past tranquil streams. A popular path is the Hermitage Walk, which takes hikers to a mysterious stone shelter known as The Hermitage, carved out of a single boulder. The forest is also home to a wide range of wildlife, making it a great spot for birdwatching and nature photography.

WATER SPORTS AND FISHING

Water Sports in Whitby

Whitby's coastal location provides an excellent setting for various water sports. Whether you're looking for a thrilling adventure or a peaceful paddle, there's something for everyone.

1. Surfing

Whitby's beaches, particularly Sandsend and Whitby Beach, are popular spots for surfing. The North Sea's waves provide the perfect conditions for both beginners and experienced surfers. Surf schools in the area offer lessons and equipment rentals, making it easy to get started.

2. Kayaking and Canoeing

Exploring Whitby's coastline by kayak or canoe is a fantastic way to see the area from a different perspective. Paddle along the rugged cliffs, discover hidden coves, and enjoy the serene waters. Kayak rentals and guided tours are available, providing a safe and enjoyable experience for all skill levels.

3. Stand-Up Paddleboarding (SUP)

Stand-up paddleboarding has become increasingly popular in Whitby. It's a great way to enjoy the calm waters and take in the stunning views. Whether you're a first-timer or an experienced paddleboarder, the local shops offer rentals and lessons to help you get started.

4. Sailing and Boating

Whitby's harbor is a hub for sailing and boating activities. You can join a sailing club, rent a boat, or take a guided tour to explore the open sea. The harbor's facilities cater to various boating needs, ensuring a pleasant experience for all.

Fishing in Whitby

Whitby has a rich fishing heritage, and it remains a favorite destination for anglers. Whether you prefer sea fishing or freshwater fishing, Whitby has plenty to offer.

1. Sea Fishing

The North Sea's abundant marine life makes sea fishing in Whitby an exciting activity. Charter a boat and head out to deeper waters to catch cod, mackerel, and haddock. Local guides and charters provide equipment and expertise to ensure a successful fishing trip.

2. Pier and Beach Fishing

If you prefer to stay closer to shore, try pier or beach fishing. Whitby's piers and beaches are ideal spots to cast your line. These areas are known for species like flounder, whiting, and bass. Bring your gear or rent from local shops and enjoy a relaxing day by the water.

3. River Fishing

The River Esk flows through Whitby and offers excellent freshwater fishing opportunities. The river is home to trout and salmon, making it a great spot for fly fishing. Ensure you have the appropriate licenses and permits, which are available from local outlets.

4. Fishing Festivals and Events

Whitby hosts various fishing festivals and events throughout the year. These gatherings celebrate the town's fishing heritage and provide a chance for anglers to compete and showcase their skills. Participating in these events is a fun way to immerse yourself in the local culture and meet fellow fishing enthusiasts.

WILDLIFE WATCHING

Coastal Cliffs and Seabirds

Whitby's coastal cliffs are home to a variety of seabirds, making it a prime spot for birdwatching. The cliffs provide nesting places for species such as kittiwakes, fulmars, and puffins. A walk along the coastal paths will show the lively activity of these birds, especially during the breeding season from April to August. Remember to bring binoculars for a closer look and enjoy the vibrant birdlife against the beautiful backdrop of the North Sea.

Whale Watching

From late summer to early fall, the waters off Whitby become a hotspot for whale sightings. Species such as minke whales, humpback whales, and even dolphins can be seen. Local boat tours offer the chance to head out to sea and experience these majestic animals in their natural habitat. These tours are not only exciting but also informative, as guides provide information about marine life and conservation efforts.

Exploring Whitby's Beaches

Whitby's beaches are teeming with sea life. Rock pooling is a popular activity, where you can find various sea creatures such as crabs, starfish, and anemones. Early mornings and late afternoons are the best times to explore the tidal pools, as the low tide shows the hidden wonders of the shore. Don't forget to wear waterproof shoes and walk lightly to protect the delicate ecosystems.

The North York Moors National Park

A short drive from Whitby, the North York Moors National Park offers a different kind of wildlife adventure. The moorlands are home to species like red grouse, curlews, and deer. The park's varied habitats, from woodlands to heather-covered moors, support a wide range of flora and fauna. Walking trails and guided tours are available to help you experience the park's natural beauty and wildlife.

The River Esk

The River Esk, which flows through Whitby, is another great spot for wildlife watching. Otters have been spotted along the riverbanks, and if you're patient and quiet, you might catch a glimpse of these secretive animals. The river is also home to kingfishers, dippers, and a range of fish species. A gentle stroll along the river path can provide plenty of chances to observe and enjoy the local wildlife.

Wildlife Conservation and Respect

While enjoying the wildlife in Whitby, it's important to respect the natural environment. Keep a safe distance from animals and their environments to avoid causing stress or harm. Follow the principles of "leave no trace" by taking all your litter with you and avoiding any actions that could disrupt the local wildlife. Supporting local conservation efforts, such as donating to wildlife charities or participating in conservation projects, can also have a positive effect.

Tips for a Successful Wildlife Watching Experience

1. Bring the Right Gear: Binoculars, a camera, and comfortable walking shoes are necessary.

2. Stay Quiet and Patient: Wildlife can be easily scared away by loud noises. Move slowly and stay calm.

3. Research and Plan: Know the best times and places for spotting different species.

4. Join a Guided Tour: Local guides have expert knowledge and can enhance your experience with their views.

5. Respect Wildlife: Maintain a safe distance and follow local rules to protect the animals and their habitats.

CHAPTER 4

CULTURAL EXPERIENCES

WHITBY FOLK WEEK

Whitby Folk Week is a lively celebration of traditional dance and music that takes place in the quaint North Yorkshire seaside town of Whitby. Thousands of people attend this yearly event, which usually takes place in August, to take part in a week full of exciting performances, seminars, and social events.

Whitby Folk Week has a range of events suitable for all age groups. There are stages all across the town where gifted singers, musicians, and dancers will perform. These performances highlight the rich cultural legacy of folk customs, ranging from upbeat ceilidh dances to melancholic songs. Unplanned acts fill the streets, bringing a lively and inviting festive atmosphere to life.

The wide range of workshops offered during Whitby Folk Week is one of its highlights. Participants can hone their current abilities or pick up new ones during these courses. Everyone can find something that interests them, whether it's learning how to play a musical instrument, honing their dancing skills, or discovering the background behind folk tunes. Experienced artists with a love for imparting their expertise and talents are leading the seminars.

Whitby Folk Week is a great place for families to go. Numerous kid-friendly events are offered, such as storytelling sessions, craft classes, and family dances. Through play and engagement, children may fully immerse themselves in the vibrant atmosphere and develop a greater understanding of folk traditions.

The festival's charm is enhanced by the town of Whitby itself. Whitby's picturesque port, an old abbey, and cobblestone streets filled with charming stores and cafes make it a lovely setting for the celebration. Discovering the town's attractions during the day and taking in the festival's activities at night combine to provide the ideal combination of sightseeing and cultural immersion for visitors.

An important part of Whitby Folk Week is the food and drink experience. Delicious alternatives ranging from gourmet delicacies to traditional fish and chips are available from local vendors. Additionally, there are pop-up cafes and bars where you may unwind, sip on a cool beverage, and take in live music.

LOCAL ART GALLERIES AND WORKSHOPS

The quaint seaside town of Whitby is home to numerous regional art studios and galleries. Your creative spirit will be stimulated by the diverse range of unique experiences offered by this dynamic community of artists and crafters.

Start your adventure with the well-liked local landmark, the Pannett Art Gallery. The gallery showcases Whitby's creativity and legacy with an excellent collection of Victorian and contemporary art. Explore its hallways to find exquisite pottery, paintings, and sculptures made by regional artists. The Pannett Art Gallery is the ideal location for appreciating this seaside town's rich artistic heritage.

Proceed to the Whitby Crafts Workshop, a central location for regional craftspeople. Watch talented artisans at work producing everything from ceramics to jewelry here. To make your stay entertaining and educational, the workshop also provides classes where you may try your hand at various crafts. Buying handcrafted mementos from local artists is an excellent way to show your support.

The Whitby Galleries is an essential destination for anyone interested in modern art. This gallery offers a venue for original and provocative artwork by showcasing shows by both established and up-and-coming artists. Every visit is unique because of the constantly rotating displays, which offer something new to view every time.

The Sutcliffe Gallery, which showcases the work of well-known Victorian photographer Frank Meadow Sutcliffe, is another noteworthy attraction. His enthralling pictures of Whitby and its residents provide an intriguing look into the town's past. The gallery is a photographers' paradise, showcasing pieces by other photographers as well.

Don't pass up the opportunity to see the fascinating process of glassblowing at the Saltwick Bay Glass Studio. The glass craftsmen at the studio produce exquisite items that vary in size from small ornaments to large sculptures. Witnessing the conversion of liquid glass into exquisite artwork is a once-in-a-lifetime event.

Lastly, have a look around the Captain Cook Memorial Museum, which honors the renowned explorer and features art exhibits about his travels and the sea. The artwork, illustrations, and objects in the museum collection depict Cook's exploits and their global influence.

LITERARY CONNECTIONS: BRAM STOKER AND DRACULA

Whitby, a quaint seaside town in North Yorkshire, England, is associated with Bram Stoker's renowned novel "Dracula," which has given it a unique place in literary history. Whitby's stunning surroundings and ominous atmosphere left a lasting impression on Stoker, who visited the town in 1890. One of history's most well-known Gothic books was written as a result of this influence.

High on the East Cliff, the ruins of Whitby Abbey are a prominent location in "Dracula." Mystery and intrigue abound in the mood created by the abbey's eerie presence and expansive vistas of the North Sea. Stoker enhanced the story's eerie aspects and sense of dread by using the abbey as a central backdrop in his book. Discover the eerie Count Dracula's first English landing scenes by exploring these historic ruins in Whitby and imagining what Stoker portrayed.

The literary history of Whitby is further enhanced by its old streets and structures. A trip into the past as well as an endurance test can be found on the 199 steps that ascend to the abbey. As you climb, picture Mina Murray and Jonathan Harker, two of the book's characters, navigating Whitby's winding lanes and historic churches. Connecting the visitor of today with Stoker's eternal invention, the ascent provides a physical relationship to the story.

Stoker spent many hours studying vampire tales and folklore from Eastern Europe, and the old library is one of Whitby's most fascinating locations. Visitors can explore the same books that stoked Stoker's imagination in the library, which is still open today. Looking through old books' pages and getting a real sense of the inspiration for "Dracula" is an intriguing experience.

Whitby Goth Weekend, an occasion that attracts enthusiasts of Gothic culture from all over the world, is another event held in the town twice a year. A colorful tribute to the Gothic culture that Stoker's writings exemplify, this event includes literature, music, and fashion. It's a fantastic chance for guests to explore the long-lasting influence of "Dracula" and become part of a community that values the dark appeal of the book.

Experiencing the local cuisine is a must-do while visiting Whitby. An authentic seaside experience may be had by eating fish and chips by the harbor while birds soar overhead. During his visit, Stoker himself may have relished in such basic pleasures, which would have given his usually spectral inspirations a hint of normalcy.

A guided tour of the town's literary past is provided by Whitby's Dracula-themed tours. Expert guides tell stories about the writing of Stoker's fabled novel, his life, and his fascination with Whitby. These trips offer a more profound comprehension of how the town's distinct personality impacted the storyline of "Dracula."

MUSIC AND THEATRE VENUES

1. Whitby Pavilion

Address: West Cliff, Whitby YO21 3EN

Description: Overlooking the North Sea, Whitby Pavilion is a historic venue that hosts a range of events, including live music, theater shows, and film screenings. The main hall, with its traditional stage and seating, offers an intimate setting for performances.

Tips: Book tickets in advance, especially during peak seasons or for famous shows. Arrive early to enjoy a walk along the nearby promenade.

Prices: Ticket prices vary based on the event, ranging from $10 to $50.

2. The Coliseum Centre

Address: Victoria Place, Whitby YO21 1EZ

Description: This community-run venue is a hub for neighborhood arts and culture. The Coliseum Centre features a cozy theater area where you can enjoy everything from drama and comedy to live music. It's a great place to experience the local talent and artistic energy of Whitby.

Tips: Check their website or local listings for future events and performances. Supporting community theaters is a wonderful way to give to the local arts scene.

Prices: Generally affordable, with tickets ranging from $8 to $30.

3. Whitby Abbey Grounds

Address: Whitby Abbey, Whitby YO22 4JT

Description: For a unique experience, attend one of the open-air concerts held on the grounds of the famous Whitby Abbey. The backdrop of the ancient ruins adds a magical atmosphere to any show. These events are particularly popular during the summer months.

Tips: Bring a blanket or lawn chair for sitting, and dress warmly for evening events as it can get chilly by the coast.

Prices: Concert ticket prices usually range from $15 to $40.

4. Whitby Yacht Club

Address: Pier Road, Whitby YO21 3PU

Description: Situated by the harbor, Whitby Yacht Club rarely hosts live music nights featuring local bands and musicians. It's a relaxed place where you can enjoy great music alongside stunning views of the harbor.

Tips: Enjoy a meal or a drink at the club's bar before the show. Check their schedule online as events can be random.

Prices: Often free entry for members; non-members may pay a small fee, normally around $5 to $10.

5. The Met Lounge and Ballroom

Address: Argyle Road, Whitby YO21 3HU

Description: This stylish club offers a mix of live music events and themed dance nights. The Met Lounge and Ballroom is known for its vibrant atmosphere and eclectic lineup, making it a popular spot for both locals and tourists.

Tips: Dress to impress for themed nights and come early for the best spots on the dance floor.

Prices: Entry fees can vary, usually ranging from $10 to $25 depending on the event.

CHAPTER 5

DINING IN WHITBY

TOP RESTAURANTS AND CAFES

1. Magpie Cafe

Location: 14 Pier Road, Whitby, YO21 3PU

Description: Magpie Cafe is famous for its fresh seafood dishes. Located near the harbor, it offers stunning views of the sea while you enjoy your meal. The interior is cozy, providing a warm atmosphere for diners.

Tips: Be sure to try the fish and chips, a local favorite. Arrive early as the cafe can get quite busy, especially during peak hours.

Prices: Main courses range from $15 to $25.

Phone Number: +44 1947 602058

2. The Moon & Sixpence

Location: Marine Parade, Whitby, YO21 3PR

Description: This modern bistro offers a mix of British and European dishes. With its stylish decor and relaxed ambiance, it's perfect for both casual lunches and romantic dinners.

Tips: Don't miss their Sunday roast, which is highly recommended. Make a reservation to secure a table, particularly on weekends.

Prices: Main courses range from $20 to $35.

Phone Number: +44 1947 604416

3. Rusty Shears

Location: 3 Silver Street, Whitby, YO21 3BU

Description: Rusty Shears is a charming cafe known for its extensive gin menu and delicious cakes. The vintage decor and garden seating make it a delightful spot for a relaxed afternoon.

Tips: The gin-tasting experience is a must-try for gin enthusiasts. Visit during the afternoon to enjoy their high tea service.

Prices: Main courses range from $10 to $20.

Phone Number: +44 1947 605383

4. Abbey Wharf

Location: Market Place, Whitby, YO22 4DD

Description: Located in the heart of Whitby, Abbey Wharf offers stunning views of the harbor and the Abbey. It specializes in seafood but also has a variety of other dishes to cater to different tastes.

Tips: Opt for a table on the balcony for the best views. You can share the seafood plate with ease.

Prices: Main courses range from $18 to $30.

Phone Number: +44 1947 606865

5. Sherlock's Coffee House

Location: 10 Flowergate, Whitby, YO21 3BA

Description: Step back in time at Sherlock's Coffee House, where the decor is inspired by the famous detective. The cozy interior and delicious homemade treats make it a popular spot for coffee lovers.

Tips: Try their scones with clotted cream and jam. It's a great place for a quiet break from exploring the town.

Prices: The cost of the main courses is $8 to $15.

Phone Number: +44 1947 825010

6. The Marine

Location: 13 Marine Parade, Whitby, YO21 3PR

Description: The Marine is an elegant restaurant with a focus on fresh, locally sourced seafood. The stylish interior and attentive service provide a memorable dining experience.

Tips: The lobster thermidor is a standout dish. Make sure to book a table in advance, especially during the summer months.

Prices: Main courses range from $25 to $40.

Phone Number: +44 1947 605022

7. Sanders Yard Bistro

Location: 95 Church Street, Whitby, YO22 4BH

Description: Located in a quaint courtyard, Sanders Yard Bistro offers a range of homemade dishes in a charming setting. It's a lovely place for breakfast, lunch, or dinner.

Tips: Their breakfast menu is extensive and very popular. Try their homemade cakes for dessert.

Prices: Main courses range from $12 to $25.

Phone Number: +44 1947 825010

8. Botham's of Whitby

Location: 8 Park Street, Whitby, YO21 1BG

Description: Botham's is a traditional bakery and cafe that has been serving Whitby since 1865. Known for its baked goods and afternoon teas, it's a must-visit for anyone with a sweet tooth.

Tips: Purchase some of their famous gingerbread to take home. Afternoon tea is a delightful experience here.

Prices: Main meals cost between $8 and $15.

Phone Number: +44 1947 602823

9. The Star Inn The Harbor

Location: Langborne Road, Whitby, YO21 1YN

Description: Offering a variety of dishes with a focus on seafood, The Star Inn The Harbor is a favorite among locals and visitors alike. The relaxed atmosphere and excellent service make it a great choice for dining.

Tips: The seafood pie is highly recommended. Reserve a table in advance, as it can get busy.

Prices: Main courses range from $20 to $35.

Phone Number: +44 1947 821900

10. Humble Pie 'n' Mash

Location: 163 Church Street, Whitby, YO22 4AS

Description: This quaint eatery specializes in traditional British pies and mash. The rustic interior and hearty meals provide a comforting dining experience.

Tips: Try the steak and ale pie, a crowd favorite. It's a good spot for a quick, satisfying meal.

Prices: Main courses range from $10 to $18.

Phone Number: +44 1947 606065

SEAFOOD SPECIALTIES

Fresh Fish and Chips

Fish and chips are a must-try in Whitby. Made with freshly caught cod or haddock, the fish is coated in a crispy batter and served with thick, golden fries. Enjoying this dish by the harbor is a typical Whitby experience. Some of the best spots to try include the Magpie Café and Quayside, where you can taste the freshest fish cooked to perfection.

Whitby Crab

Whitby is famous for its succulent crab, a local treat. Whether eaten in a salad, as part of a seafood platter, or in a simple crab sandwich, the sweet, tender meat is a treat. The Fortune's Kippers shop is a great place to find delicious, freshly made crab dishes.

Smoked Kippers

Smoked kippers are another highlight of Whitby. These are herring that have been split, salted, and smoked over oak chips, giving them a rich, smoky taste. Fortune's Kippers, a family-run business since 1872, is the best place to try this classic treat. A visit to their smokehouse is a step back in time and a chance to enjoy one of Whitby's oldest culinary traditions.

Scallops

The North Sea offers Whitby with some of the finest scallops. These delicate shellfish are often served pan-seared with a simple dressing of salt, pepper, and a squeeze of lemon juice. Many local restaurants, such as The Marine and Abbey Wharf, offer carefully prepared scallop dishes that highlight their natural sweetness.

Mussels

Whitby's mussels are taken from the nearby coast and are a popular dish in local eateries. Often cooked in white wine and garlic sauce, they are served steaming hot with toasted bread. The Moon and Sixpence offer a delightful mussel dish that gets the essence of Whitby's seafood offerings.

Lobster

Lobster is a prized catch in Whitby, known for its firm, delicious meat. It is often served simply, with melted butter and a squeeze of lemon, allowing the freshness of the lobster to shine through. The Star Inn the Harbor is a great place to enjoy a luxurious lobster meal while viewing the beautiful Whitby harbor.

Cullen Skink

This hearty Scottish soup, made with smoked haddock, potatoes, and onions, has found its way into the hearts of Whitby's residents and tourists. It's a comforting dish that warms you up on a cool seaside evening. Many local bars and restaurants, like Humble Pie 'n' Mash, offer their take on this flavorful soup.

Seafood Platters

For those who want to taste a bit of everything, seafood platters are an excellent choice. These often include a range of shellfish, smoked fish, and fresh catches of the day, giving a comprehensive taste of Whitby's seafood bounty. The Marine offers an impressive seafood platter that shows the diversity and quality of the town's offerings.

PUBS AND BREWERIES

1. The Whitby Brewery

Located at East Cliff, the Whitby Brewery is a must-visit for beer lovers. Nestled at the base of Whitby Abbey, this brewery offers a range of handmade ales that reflect the spirit of the town. Prices run from $5 to $7 per pint. You can enjoy a tour of the brewery for a small fee, which includes a taste session. For more information, call (01947) 601982.

2. The Black Horse Inn

Situated on Church Street, The Black Horse Inn is one of Whitby's oldest pubs, rich in history and charm. This traditional pub offers a range of local ales and classic pub fare. With a cozy atmosphere, it's an ideal place to unwind after a day of sightseeing. Prices for drinks run from $4 to $6. To reach them, dial (01947) 602906.

3. The Station Inn

The Station Inn, located on New Quay Road, is a famous spot among both locals and tourists. Known for its friendly service and extensive range of cask ales, this pub also offers live music on weekends. Prices are quite affordable, with most drinks costing between $5 and $8. For questions, call (01947) 820565.

4. The Fleece

Found on Church Street, The Fleece is a friendly pub that boasts stunning views of the harbor. Offering a wide range of beers, including some unique craft brews, it's a great place to relax and enjoy the view. Prices for drinks run from $4 to $7. For more details, call them at (01947) 603005.

5. The Endeavour

The Endeavour, located on Grape Lane, is a cozy bar known for its warm atmosphere and friendly staff. This pub offers a range of Whitby's finest ales and ciders. Prices range from $4 to $6. It's a great spot to enjoy a quiet evening with friends. You can reach them at (01947) 606172.

6. The Dolphin Hotel

Situated on Bridge Street, The Dolphin Hotel offers not only comfortable accommodation but also a lively pub environment. With a selection of local and international beers, this spot is great for those looking to enjoy a drink with a view of the river. Prices range from $5 to $8. For more information, call (01947) 821455.

7. Little Angel

Located on Flowergate, Little Angel is known for its extensive beer range and vibrant ambiance. This bar frequently hosts events and live music, making it a lively spot to visit. Drinks are charged between $5 and $8. Contact them at (01947) 820475 for more information.

8. The Granby

Found on Skinner Street, The Granby is a traditional bar offering a friendly atmosphere and a great range of local ales. It's a favorite among locals for its cozy setting and affordable prices, with drinks running from $4 to $6. For more information, call (01947) 601747.

VEGAN AND VEGETARIAN OPTIONS

1. The Greens

Location: 14 St. Ann's Staith, Whitby

Description: The Greens is a popular spot for plant-based meals. Their menu includes a variety of vegan and vegetarian dishes, such as the delicious roasted vegetable lasagna and their famous lentil and vegetable pie. The ambiance is cozy, and the staff is friendly, making it a great place for a relaxed meal.

Prices: Main courses range from $12 to $18.

Phone Number: +44 1947 602110

2. Humphrey's

Location: 2 Baxtergate, Whitby

Description: Humphrey's is known for its creative vegetarian and vegan menu. From their hearty chickpea and spinach curry to mouthwatering vegan burgers, there's something for everyone. They also offer a selection of vegan desserts, including a rich chocolate torte.

Prices: Main dishes range from $10 to $16.

Phone Number: +44 1947 821800

3. Trenchers

Location: New Quay Road, Whitby

Description: Trenchers is famous for its fresh seafood, but it also has a fantastic selection of vegetarian and vegan options. Try their vegan fish and chips, made with banana blossom, or their hearty vegetable stew. The restaurant offers a pleasant atmosphere with views of the harbor.

Prices: Main courses range from $14 to $20.

Phone Number: +44 1947 603212

4. The Moon and Sixpence

Location: Marine Parade, Whitby

Description: This stylish bistro offers a variety of vegetarian and vegan dishes. Highlights include the roasted beetroot and quinoa salad and the delicious vegan shepherd's pie. The Moon and Sixpence also has a great selection of vegan wines and cocktails.

Prices: Main dishes range from $15 to $22.

Phone Number: +44 1947 604416

5. Humble Pie 'n' Mash

Location: 163 Church Street, Whitby

Description: This quaint eatery specializes in traditional British pies with a vegan twist. Their vegan pie, filled with mushrooms, leeks, and herbs, is a must-try. Pair it with mashed potatoes and gravy for a comforting meal. The cozy setting and friendly service make it a favorite among locals and visitors alike.

Prices: Pies range from $8 to $12.

Phone Number: +44 1947 606222

6. Sherlock's Coffee House

Location: 10 Flowergate, Whitby

Description: Sherlock's Coffee House is a delightful spot for a light meal or snack. They offer a variety of vegan and vegetarian sandwiches, soups, and salads. Don't miss their vegan chocolate cake, which pairs perfectly with a cup of freshly brewed coffee.

Prices: Light meals range from $6 to $10.

Phone Number: +44 1947 821530

7. Rusty Shears

Location: 3 Silver Street, Whitby

Description: Rusty Shears is a quirky café offering a range of vegan and vegetarian dishes. From their hearty vegan breakfast to their delicious plant-based wraps and sandwiches, there's plenty to choose from. The garden seating area is a lovely spot to enjoy your meal.

Prices: Main dishes range from $8 to $15.

Phone Number: +44 1947 603230

8. Ditto Restaurant

Location: 26 Skinner Street, Whitby

Description: Ditto is a small, family-run restaurant with a focus on quality and flavor. Their vegetarian and vegan options include dishes like butternut squash risotto and a delightful vegetable tagine. The intimate setting and excellent service make it a great choice for a special meal.

Prices: Main courses range from $16 to $24.

Phone Number: +44 1947 601404

CHAPTER 6

SHOPPING AND SOUVENIRS

LOCAL MARKETS AND SHOPS

1. Whitby Market

Located in the heart of the town, Whitby Market is a must-visit for both locals and tourists. This open-air market runs every Monday, Wednesday, Friday, and Saturday. You can find a range of goods, from fresh produce and homemade crafts to antiques and clothes. Prices are quite reasonable, with fresh produce starting at around $1 per item and handmade crafts ranging from $5 to $50. For more information, call (01287) 619622.

2. The Whitby Bookshop

For book fans, The Whitby Bookshop on Church Street is a gem. This independent bookstore gives a wide selection of new and second-hand books across various genres. Prices range from $5 to $30, based on the book's condition and rarity. They also host rare author events and book signings. Contact them at (01947) 606202 for more information.

3. Whitby Deli

If you're looking for gourmet treats and local sweets, head to Whitby Deli on Flowergate. This lovely shop sells an array of fine cheeses, cured meats, artisanal bread, and local preserves. Prices for deli foods start at around $3.50. They also offer gift hampers that are great for special occasions. Call (01947) 229900 for more information.

4. The Shepherd's Purse

Located on Church Street, The Shepherd's Purse offers a range of unique gifts and natural products. From handmade soaps and skincare items to jewelry and home decor, there's something for everyone. Prices range from $5 for small things to $50 for more elaborate pieces. Reach out to them at (01947) 820835.

5. Whitby Wool & Craft Shop

Crafters will enjoy a visit to the Whitby Wool & Craft Shop on Skinner Street. This shop offers a wide range of yarns, knitting supplies, and craft kits. Prices start at $2 for small things like needles and go up to $40 for premium yarns and kits. For more information, call (01947) 821347.

6. The Whitby Jet Heritage Centre

On Church Street, you'll find The Whitby Jet Heritage Centre, a perfect place to buy Whitby's famous jet jewelry. The shop offers a variety of handcrafted jet pieces, from simple earrings starting at $20 to intricate necklaces costing up to $200. For more information, call (01947) 603331.

7. The Green Dragon

Located on Grape Lane, The Green Dragon offers a range of eco-friendly and fair-trade products. From clothing and accessories to household items and gifts, everything is sustainably made. Prices vary from $10 for small items to $100 for bigger pieces. Call (01947) 602828 for further questions.

8. The Endeavour Stores

Situated on the east side of Whitby, The Endeavour Stores provide a range of local produce, including fresh seafood, meats, and veggies. Prices are reasonable, with seafood starting at $5 per pound and meats at $4 per pound. For more information, call (01947) 820973.

ARTISANAL CRAFTS AND GIFTS

Whitby is a sanctuary for connoisseurs of handcrafted goods and unusual presents. The handcrafted goods made by regional artisans capture the town's colorful culture and rich heritage. These handcrafted goods provide a tangible piece of Whitby that can be brought home and make ideal gifts and souvenirs.

The Whitby Craft and Gift Shop is a great spot to begin your exploration. This shop, which is located in the center of town, sells a range of handcrafted goods, including ceramics and jewelry. Every item is expertly made, showcasing the artisan's talent and enthusiasm. The store, where you can meet the makers and discover more about their skills, is renowned for its welcoming atmosphere.

It is essential for everyone interested in textiles to visit the Whitby Wool Shop. This welcoming shop has a large assortment of homemade knitted items and wool that is acquired locally. You may find items to keep you warm throughout the winter, such as comfy scarves and stylish sweaters. For those who enjoy crafts, the store is a terrific place to stop because it also sells knitting supplies and patterns.

The Whitby Jet Jewelry stores have very unusual items if you're looking for them. Whitby is well-known for its jet, a fossilized wood that has been utilized for generations in jewelry-making. Beautiful pieces, ranging from delicate earrings to dramatic necklaces, are crafted by the town's jewelers. Every jewelry item made of jet serves as a lovely memento of Whitby's natural heritage and artistry.

Art enthusiasts shouldn't miss the Whitby Gallery, which features artwork from regional artists. The gallery showcases a variety of mediums, such as photographs, sculptures, and paintings. Numerous items perfectly encapsulate Whitby, making them ideal keepsakes for your trip. Meet the artists and discover more about their work at the gallery's frequent events and shows.

The Whitby Market is a gold mine for people who value handcrafted home products. The market, which is held once a week, has vendors offering anything from carved wooden objects to handmade candles. It's a terrific spot to discover unique items that bring a little Whitby into your house. You can have a fantastic conversation about techniques and inspirations with local artisans at the market.

Remember to stop by the Whitby Pottery Studio, where you can watch potters in action and even have a go at creating your creations. All ages will enjoy the workshops and classes that the studio offers. This shop produces a variety of ceramics, from beautiful pieces that look excellent as gifts to useful goods like bowls and mugs.

And last, a visit to the Whitby Bookshop is a must for all readers. This quaint bookshop has a carefully chosen collection of books, many written by or about Whitby-based authors. Everything from modern literature to historical novels may be found, all of which honor the town's illustrious literary past. The bookstore also offers opportunities to interact with the local literary community through readings and signings.

WHITBY JET JEWELRY

Whitby Jet Jewelry is one of the most treasured things you can find when visiting the coastal town of Whitby. Known for its deep black color and rich history, the Whitby jet has been a sought-after material for ages, especially during the Victorian era when it became famous for mourning jewelry.

History and Significance

Whitby jet is a type of lignite, formed from the fossilized wood of the Araucaria tree that grew in the area around 180 million years ago. This unique gemstone has been used for ornamental reasons since prehistoric times. The Romans were the first to craft it into jewelry, but it was during the Victorian time that the Whitby jet reached its peak popularity. Queen Victoria, mourning the death of Prince Albert, set a trend by wearing jet jewelry, which symbolizes mourning and purity.

Craftsmanship and Quality

The craftsmanship involved in making Whitby jet jewelry is both intricate and skilled. Local artisans carefully pick the jet, which is then shaped, polished, and often combined with precious metals like silver and gold. The result is stunning pieces that range from brooches and pendants to rings and bangles. Each piece is unique, showing the natural beauty of the jet and the skill of the jeweler.

Where to Find Whitby Jet Jewelry

Whitby is home to several famous shops and galleries where you can find exquisite jet jewelry. These establishments not only sell beautiful pieces but also offer insights into the past and process of jet jewelry making. Some famous places include:

1. W Hamond Jewellers: Established in 1860, W Hamond is one of the oldest and most famous jet jewelers in Whitby. The shop offers a wide range of handmade jet jewelry and also has a museum where you can learn more about the history of Whitby Jet.

2. The Jet Store: Located in the heart of Whitby, The Jet Store features an amazing collection of jet jewelry. The store prides itself on using traditional methods to make contemporary designs.

3. Ebor Jetworks: This family-run business specializes in custom jet jewelry. They offer a variety of unique designs and are happy to make custom pieces upon request.

Tips for Purchasing Whitby Jet Jewelry

When buying Whitby jet jewelry, it's important to ensure you are getting genuine Whitby jet. Here are a few tips:

1. Check for validity: Reputable shops will provide certificates of validity. Make sure to ask for one when making a buy.

2. Inspect the Quality: The genuine Whitby jet should have a smooth, glass-like shine. Beware of imitations that might look similar but lack the quality and durability of a real Whitby jet.

3. Understand the Value: The price of Whitby jet jewelry can change based on the size, quality, and craftsmanship. Do some study to understand the market value before making a purchase.

Why Choose Whitby Jet Jewelry?

Owning a piece of Whitby jet jewelry is like owning a piece of history. The deep black gemstone, with its mysterious and timeless charm, makes for a striking addition to any jewelry collection. Moreover, the craftsmanship involved ensures that each piece is special and made to last. Whether as a gift or a personal keepsake, Whitby jet jewelry is a meaningful and beautiful reminder of Whitby's rich history.

BOOKSTORES AND ANTIQUES

Bookstores in Whitby

Whitby Bookshop: Located in the heart of the town, Whitby Bookshop is a must-visit for book fans. The independent bookstore offers a wide range of books, from classic literature to modern fiction. The shop's experienced staff are always ready to help you find the perfect read. With its inviting atmosphere and well-curated range, Whitby Bookshop is the ideal place to spend a leisurely afternoon exploring the world of books.

The Whitby Literary & Philosophical Society Library: This historic library, formed in the early 19th century, is home to an impressive collection of rare books, manuscripts, and local archives. It's a haven for researchers and history enthusiasts looking to dig into Whitby's past. The library also hosts regular events, including author talks and book signings, making it a lively cultural hub in the town.

Barnby's Books: A quaint second-hand bookstore, Barnby's Books is great for those who enjoy browsing through shelves of pre-loved books. The store features an eclectic mix of genres, from vintage books to modern bestsellers, ensuring there's something for everyone. The friendly owner is always eager to chat about books and offer recommendations based on your interests.

Antique Shops in Whitby

Robinsons Antiques: Situated near the harbor, Robinsons Antiques offers an interesting array of antiques and collectibles. From Victorian furniture to delicate porcelain, this shop is a treasure trove for antique lovers. The carefully curated items show Whitby's rich heritage, making it a wonderful place to find unique souvenirs or gifts.

Black Market Antiques: Located on Flowergate, Black Market Antiques specializes in vintage jewelry, clocks, and artifacts. The shop's collection is constantly changing, so each visit offers discoveries. Whether you're a seasoned collector or a curious visitor, Black Market Antiques offers a glimpse into the past through its diverse range of items.

Georgian Antiques & Collectables: This charming store offers a wide selection of Georgian-era antiques, including fine china, silverware, and artwork. The shop's knowledgeable staff are passionate about the past of each piece and are happy to share their expertise. It's a delightful place to find a piece of Whitby's past to take home with you.

Tips for Visiting

1. Explore on Foot: Whitby's bookstores and antique shops are best explored on foot, allowing you to take in the town's scenic beauty and find hidden gems along the way.

2. Check Opening Hours: Some shops have limited opening hours, especially during the off-peak season. It's a good idea to make sure you don't miss anything by checking ahead of time.

3. Engage with Locals: The shop owners and staff are often locals with a wealth of information about Whitby. Never be afraid to start a conversation and request recommendations.

CHAPTER 7

FAMILY FUN

KID-FRIENDLY ATTRACTIONS

Begin your journey with the magnificent remains of Whitby Abbey, steeped in history. Kids will enjoy exploring the historic ruins and discovering the local folklore. Children can run around and burn off some steam in the abundant area provided by the monastery, which boasts stunning vistas. Check out the visitor center as well; with its interactive exhibits and activities, history is brought to life for people of all ages.

After that, visit the Whitby Museum for an intriguing look into the town's history. Exhibits spanning natural history and fossils to model ships and nautical items can be seen throughout the museum. Youngsters will find the interactive exhibits and the chance to discover Whitby's history of fishing and whaling especially fascinating.

Visit Pannett Park for some outdoor recreation. This exquisitely designed park offers plenty of open areas for games and picnics, as well as gardens and a kids' play area. Additionally, the Pannett Art Gallery is located in the park and features artwork by regional artists. The kids can play as you unwind and take in the fresh air.

Without going to the beach, a trip to Whitby is not complete. Whitby Beach's pristine seas, rock pools, and sandy coastlines make it an ideal family destination. Youngsters can go shell hunting, paddle in the sea, and make sandcastles. It's simple to get to the beach using the nearby West Cliff Lift, especially if you're carrying strollers or little children.

Take the family on a boat ride from Whitby Harbor for an exciting and different experience. Numerous tours, such as whale-watching journeys, fishing outings, and picturesque cruises, are offered. Enjoy the breathtaking views of the coast and get up close and personal with marine life during these boat rides.

The Whitby Lifeboat Station is another important site to see. The public can view this operational lifeboat station, which offers an intriguing look into the critical work done by the RNLI. The lifeboats and equipment on exhibit will captivate children, and they can also educate them about the courageous volunteers who put their lives in danger to save others at sea.

A trip to the Dracula Experience is essential if your children enjoy scary stories. Whitby served as inspiration for the plot of Bram Stoker's well-known novel, which is told in this interactive display. For older kids, the story is brought to life in a lighthearted and slightly eerie fashion through the use of real performers, special effects, and intricate sets.

The SEA LIFE Scarborough, which caters to marine enthusiasts, is conveniently located a short drive from Whitby. Sea life abounds at this aquarium, including turtles, penguins, sharks, and rays. Children can interact with starfish and crabs in the interactive rockpool, and the regular feeding demonstrations are always a big attraction.

The North Yorkshire Moors Railway journey is something you shouldn't pass up, to sum up. With breathtaking trips through the stunning North York Moors National Park, this historic steam railway is available. Kids will adore the thrill of riding on a vintage steam train, and it's a great opportunity to see the countryside.

FAMILY ACTIVITIES AND EVENTS

Explore Whitby Abbey: The famous Whitby Abbey, perched high on the East Cliff, is a must-visit. Kids will love the adventure of climbing the 199 steps to reach the abbey ruins, where they can learn about the site's past through interactive exhibits. The panoramic views of Whitby from the top are stunning.

Discover the Dracula Connection: For families with older kids, discovering Whitby's connection to Bram Stoker's Dracula is a thrilling experience. You can visit the Dracula Experience, a unique museum that brings the famous book to life with dramatic displays and sound effects.

Enjoy Whitby Beach: Whitby's sandy beaches are great for a day of relaxation and play. Build sandcastles, paddle in the sea, or simply enjoy lunch with the family. Don't forget to try some classic fish and chips from one of the seaside vendors.

Visit the Captain Cook Memorial Museum: Learn about the life and voyages of Captain James Cook at this fascinating museum housed in the house where Cook lodged as an apprentice. The museum offers engaging exhibits and activities for children, making history fun and informative.

Take a Boat Trip: Experience Whitby from the water by taking a boat trip along the coast. Various operators offer trips ranging from short harbor tours to longer coastal excursions, giving a unique perspective of the town and its surroundings.

Participate in the Whitby Regatta: If you're coming in August, the Whitby Regatta is an event not to be missed. This historic maritime festival includes boat races, a funfair, fireworks, and a grand parade. Everything to keep the whole family occupied is available.

Explore Pannett Park: Pannett Park is a beautiful green area in the heart of Whitby, perfect for family outings. The park includes a children's playground, a lily pond, and the Whitby Museum, which has a variety of exhibits that kids will find interesting.

Ride the North Yorkshire Moors Railway: Take a beautiful steam train ride through the stunning North York Moors National Park. The North Yorkshire Moors Railway offers a nostalgic journey that both kids and adults will enjoy, with the chance to see beautiful landscapes and wildlife.

Attend the Whitby Goth Weekend: For something special, plan your visit around the Whitby Goth Weekend, held twice a year. This event features live music, markets, and plenty of people in elaborate costumes, making it a fun and visually exciting experience for children.

Explore the Whitby Wizard: This interactive science museum is great for curious minds. The Whitby Wizard offers hands-on exhibits and experiments that make learning about science entertaining and interesting for children.

PARKS AND PLAYGROUNDS

Whitby is a fun family destination with lots of parks and playgrounds to make sure the whole family has a nice time. Whitby has something for everyone, whether you're searching for a location to have a family picnic or a place for the kids to play.

Pannett Park, which is in the center of Whitby, is one of the attractions. This lovely green area is ideal for a family trip. It has lots of space for a stroll, well-kept plants, and a kid's play area. With its swings, slides, and climbing frames, the playground offers kids countless hours of entertainment. In addition, there's a charming pond where you can take in the serene surroundings and see ducks.

Whitby Abbey Grounds is another fantastic location. The grounds around the abbey provide plenty of space for children to run around and explore, even though it is mostly recognized for its historical value. This is a great spot for a family picnic with breathtaking views. The open area is a favored spot for both locals and tourists because it permits a variety of outdoor games and activities.

Go to West Cliff Beach for a relaxing time by the water. This sandy area is great for playing beach games, making sandcastles, or just lounging in the sea wind. The adjacent Captain Cook Memorial Museum is also well worth a trip, providing the whole family with enjoyable educational activities.

Whitby has several smaller playgrounds dotted about the community. One well-liked option is the play area at Whitby Leisure Centre. It makes sure that every child has something to enjoy by providing contemporary play equipment appropriate for a range of age groups.

Visit the Cinder Track, a beautiful trail that was formerly a railroad line, for a little adventure and nature. It's ideal for family exploration, cycling, and walking. There are places to stop along the route and enjoy the breathtaking views of the surrounding landscape and ocean.

Lastly, make sure to visit Ruswarp Pleasure Boats. Canoes and rowboats are available for hire at this location, which is only a short drive from Whitby. Enjoying the peace of the river while canoeing along it is a great way to pass a sunny afternoon.

CHAPTER 8

EVENTS AND FESTIVALS

ANNUAL EVENTS CALENDAR

Whitby Goth Weekend

This bi-annual fair, held in April and October, is one of Whitby's most famous events. It draws goths from all over the world. Expect live music, markets, and a friendly, welcoming scene. It's a great chance to see some incredible costumes and enjoy the vibrant nightlife.

Whitby Regatta

Taking place every August, the Whitby Regatta is a three-day event that combines rowing races, a funfair, and different entertainment activities. The event concludes with a spectacular fireworks display over the harbor, making it an unforgettable experience for visitors of all ages.

Whitby Folk Week

In late August, Whitby Folk Week celebrates traditional music, dance, and stories. The town comes alive with performances, workshops, and sessions in various venues, making it a wonderful time to explore and enjoy Whitby's rich cultural history.

Whitby 60s Festival

This nostalgic event, held in June, brings back the sounds and styles of the 1960s. Enjoy live bands, dance events, and themed activities that capture the spirit of this famous decade. It's a fun-filled weekend that draws to all generations.

Whitby Fish and Ships Festival

Celebrating the town's maritime history, this festival in May highlights Whitby's fishing business and culinary delights. With cooking demonstrations, seafood tastings, and maritime-themed entertainment, it's a must-visit for food lovers and history fans alike.

Whitby Christmas Festival

Kicking off the holiday season in late November, the Whitby Christmas Festival features a bustling market, live entertainment, and the switching on of the Christmas lights. It's a magical time to visit, with the town decked out in holiday decorations and plenty of chances for festive shopping.

Whitby Krampus Run

In early December, Whitby hosts a unique event inspired by the myth of Krampus. Participants dress in elaborate outfits to parade through the town, creating a lively and somewhat eerie spectacle.

It's an event that shows Whitby's love for quirky and unusual traditions.

WHITBY GOTH WEEKEND

A unique event, Whitby Goth Weekend takes place twice a year in the picturesque village of Whitby, England. This festival draws attendees from all around the world and has grown to be a major event for the goth subculture. During these weekends, Whitby, a town well-known for its breathtaking seaside views and historic sites, comes alive with gothic culture.

Since its founding in 1994, Whitby Goth Weekend has developed into one of the most well-known goth gatherings in the world. It happens between April and October when the town's natural beauty and ambiance are at their peak. Whether you're a die-hard goth or just interested in the culture, you can attend the event.

Whitby Goth Weekend's varied live music schedule is its main attraction. Bands from all around the town play in various venues, featuring styles such as punk, alternative, and goth. These shows provide a warm, inviting atmosphere that is ideal for dancing and just listening to the music.

The festival includes a sizable market with exhibitors offering gothic-style apparel, accessories, and artwork in addition to the music. This market is a veritable gold mine for anyone searching for unusual products that embody the gothic vibe. Everything from intricate costumes to artisan jewelry is available for everybody to enjoy.

The amazing costumes worn by participants during Whitby Goth Weekend are among its most noticeable features. Individuals dress in lavish gothic fashion, ranging from contemporary punk ensembles to Victorian-inspired gowns. The town transforms into a spectacle as people display their originality and sense of flair. This results in a visually stunning experience where every street and corner is teeming with life and personality.

Whitby itself has a lot to discover. Fans of Bram Stoker's "Dracula," who are familiar with the area, will relish touring the recognizable Whitby Abbey and the 199 stairs that lead up to it. The weekend's gothic vibe is enhanced by the Abbey, which is situated atop a hill with a view of the town. Whitby's winding lanes, filled with eccentric stores and quaint cafés, make the ideal setting for this unusual celebration.

Whitby Goth Weekend attendees must make advance plans. It is advised to reserve your accommodations in Whitby in advance of the event since they tend to fill up quickly. There are plenty of options to suit every budget, ranging from charming bed & breakfasts to more opulent hotels.

Whitby has a wide variety of restaurants and cafes for dining, making it a delightful experience. Numerous places welcome the gothic motif, offering a lively and engaging dining experience. There are many options to suit your palate, whether you're in the mood for a classic British meal or something more exotic.

Whitby Goth Weekend is a celebration of a lively and diverse community rather than just a festival. People from different walks of life may come together and enjoy a common passion at the event, which promotes a sense of acceptance and belonging. It is made sure that everyone feels valued and included in the friendly environment.

MARITIME FESTIVALS

Whitby Regatta

The Whitby Regatta, one of the oldest sea regattas on the northeast coast of England, is a highlight of the town's summer schedule. Held annually in August, the regatta spans three days filled with different activities and events. From rowing races in the picturesque harbor to a grand fireworks show that lights up the night sky, the regatta offers something for everyone. Families can enjoy funfair rides, food stalls, and entertainment while watching the exciting boat races. The event is a perfect blend of competition, community energy, and seaside fun.

Whitby Folk Week

Whitby Folk Week, held every August, turns the town into a lively hub of music and dance. This week-long event celebrates traditional folk music and dance, drawing performers and enthusiasts from all over the country. With over 600 events, including concerts, workshops, and ceilidhs, there's never a dull time. The festival takes place in different venues around Whitby, from the beautiful seaside to historic buildings, creating a lively and festive atmosphere. Visitors can join in workshops to learn traditional dances or simply enjoy the performances.

Whitby Goth Weekend

Whitby Goth Weekend, a bi-annual event held in April and October, is one of the world's top goth music festivals. The event brings together goths, steampunk, and alternative music fans for a weekend of live music, special markets, and social events. The festival celebrates Whitby's connection to Bram Stoker's Dracula, with many attendees dressing in elaborate costumes inspired by the gothic book. The unique atmosphere and striking outfits make it a must-see event for anyone visiting Whitby.

Whitby Fish & Ships Festival

The Whitby Fish & Ships Festival is a relatively new addition to the town's festival scene, celebrating Whitby's maritime history and its status as a fishing port. Held in May, the event includes cooking demonstrations from famous chefs, seafood tastings, and maritime-themed entertainment. Visitors can learn about the fishing industry's past, watch traditional boat building, and enjoy music and street theater. The festival displays the best of Whitby's seafood and maritime culture, making it a delicious and educational experience.

Whitby 60s Festival

For those who love the music and society of the 1960s, the Whitby 60s Festival is a must-visit event. Held in June, the event includes live performances from tribute bands, dance nights, and themed markets. Attendees can enjoy the retro atmosphere, dressing up in 60s fashion and dancing to classic hits. The festival takes place at different venues around the town, adding a lively and colorful vibe to Whitby's summer scene.

FOOD AND DRINK FESTIVALS

The Whitby Food and Drink Festival, which takes place every summer, is one of the highlights. A variety of locally produced goods are on display at this fair, such as freshly caught fish, handmade cheeses, and handcrafted drinks. Aside from taking part in cooking demos and exploring a variety of vendors selling delectable sweets, visitors can also take in live music that enhances the festive mood. In addition, the festival offers workshops where guests can pick up new cooking skills and recipes from well-known chefs.

Another event that is not to be missed is the Whitby Fish and Ships Festival. This festival honors the town's marine history and is centered around seafood and traditional maritime crafts. Freshest catches from nearby fishermen are brought in, and skilled cooks transform them into creative yet classic meals. The festival is a fantastic family-friendly event that also features boat exhibitions, marine speakers, and craft workshops.

The Whitby Beer Festival is ideal for people who enjoy a great ale. This event, which takes place at the historic Whitby Pavilion, features a large assortment of beers, ciders, and spirits from the area. While enjoying live entertainment, such as musicians and local entertainers, attendees can sample a variety of beers. It's a well-liked event for both residents and visitors because of the lively and welcoming atmosphere.

Although it is a more recent addition to the town's festival schedule, the Whitby Gin and Prosecco Festival has grown in popularity quite quickly. A wide selection of gins and proseccos from domestic and foreign suppliers are available at this event. Indulge in tastings, discover the origins and manufacturing processes of these libations, and savor food combinations that are intended to combine with them. This event is a great experience because of the live music and laid-back atmosphere.

Whitby's Christmas Market and Food Festival blends the town's delicious food with the joyous atmosphere of the holidays. This December celebration turns the town into a winter paradise complete with vendors selling holiday gifts, handcrafted goods, and seasonal cuisine. While looking through the unusual gifts, guests can enjoy classic holiday fare like mulled wine, mince pies, and roasted chestnuts.

CHAPTER 9

DAY TRIPS AND EXCURSIONS

NEARBY COASTAL VILLAGES

Robin Hood's Bay

A short drive south of Whitby, Robin Hood's Bay is a beautiful town known for its steep, narrow streets and stunning views. The town is rich in history and was once a hotspot for smugglers. Today, you can explore its cobbled streets, visit local shops, and enjoy fresh fish at the village's cozy pubs and restaurants. The beach is perfect for fossil hunting and rock pooling, making it a fun location for families.

Staithes

North of Whitby lies Staithes, a village that has kept its traditional fishing village charm. Staithes is famous for its art scene, inspired by its beautiful harbor and rugged rocks. Wander through the winding alleys, visit the local galleries, and enjoy a meal at one of the seafood places. The Staithes Heritage Center and Captain Cook Museum offer a glimpse into the village's maritime past and its link to the famous explorer.

Runswick Bay

Just a few miles from Staithes, Runswick Bay is another gem on the Yorkshire coast. This town offers a tranquil escape with its sandy beach and quaint cottages. It's an ideal spot for a relaxed walk along the coast or a peaceful day by the sea. The bay is also a favorite among kayakers and sailors, giving a serene setting for water sports. Don't forget to visit the Runswick Bay Rescue Boat station, which has been saving lives since 1982.

Sandsend

Sandsend is a small town located just a couple of miles from Whitby. It's known for its expansive beach, which is great for a relaxing day out. Take a walk along the sands, explore the rock pools, or enjoy a coffee at one of the beachside cafes. Sandsend is also the starting point for a scenic walk along the Cleveland Way, which offers amazing views of the coastline.

Saltburn-by-the-Sea

A bit further away, Saltburn-by-the-Sea is worth the journey. This Victorian seaside resort boasts a long pier, beautiful gardens, and a cliff lift that offers panoramic views of the coast. Saltburn is also popular with surfers, and its wide beach is great for a variety of water sports. The Saltburn Cliff Tramway is a unique attraction, being one of the oldest water-powered funiculars still in service.

Flamborough Head

While a bit of a drive from Whitby, Flamborough Head gives dramatic coastal scenery that is well worth the trip. The headland is known for its white chalk rocks, which provide a striking contrast to the blue sea. It's a great place for hikes, birdwatching, and photography. Visit the Flamborough Lighthouse for spectacular views and learn about the area's maritime past.

Robin Hoods Bay to Ravenscar

For those who enjoy hiking, the path from Robin Hood's Bay to Ravenscar is a must. This part of the Cleveland Way offers stunning views of the North Sea and the rugged coastline. The route is about 7 miles long and takes you through beautiful scenery, including moorland and cliffs. Ravenscar, known as the "town that never was," offers intriguing ruins and a fascinating past.

NORTH YORK MOORS NATIONAL PARK

The North York Moors National Park, a short drive from Whitby, offers a variety of activities and experiences great for a day trip. With its sweeping moorland, quaint villages, and historic landmarks, this park offers an unforgettable adventure.

Begin your day with a visit to Goathland, a charming town famous for its role in the TV series "Heartbeat" and as Hogsmeade Station in the "Harry Potter" films. Stroll through the town, take in the rustic charm, and perhaps enjoy a cup of tea at one of the local cafes.

Next, head to the North Yorkshire Moors Railway, one of the world's most scenic heritage trains. The steam trains run through the heart of the park, offering breathtaking views of the moors and forests. A ride on this railway is like stepping back in time, offering a unique way to see the area.

For wildlife enthusiasts, the moors themselves are a highlight. The expansive heather-covered landscapes change with the seasons, giving beautiful views and peaceful walking trails. Consider a hike along the Cleveland Way, which offers stunning views and a chance to see local wildlife.

Explore the charming town of Helmsley, known for its historic castle and vibrant market square. Helmsley Castle, with its impressive ruins and informative displays, gives a glimpse into the region's rich past. The village also has lovely shops and eateries where you can taste local delicacies.

Rievaulx Abbey, a short drive from Helmsley, is another must-visit. This impressive ruin of a former Cistercian monastery is set in a tranquil valley and gives insight into the lives of medieval monks. The on-site museum and audio tours enrich your understanding of this historic spot.

For those who enjoy outdoor activities, Dalby Forest is an excellent location. This expansive forest offers biking tracks, walking walks, and picnic spots. The brave can try the Go Ape treetop adventure course, which includes zip lines and high ropes.

And your day with a visit to the coastal town of Robin Hood's Bay. This quaint town, with its narrow streets and historic cottages, is great for a leisurely walk. The beach is a great spot for fossil finding, and the local pubs offer hearty meals to round off your day.

HISTORIC SITES IN THE REGION

Robin Hood's Bay

Just a short drive from Whitby, Robin Hood's Bay is a charming fishing town with narrow streets and old buildings. Walk through the cobbled paths, visit the local museum, and enjoy the beautiful views of the coast. It's a great spot to learn about the area's smuggling history.

Rievaulx Abbey

A trip to Rievaulx Abbey is a journey back in time. This impressive ruin of a Cistercian abbey is set in a tranquil valley near Helmsley. Wander through the remains of the abbey, and picture the monks' lives here in the 12th century. The tourist center offers interesting exhibits and a café with lovely views.

Castle Howard

Castle Howard, one of England's most beautiful stately homes, is within an hour's drive of Whitby. Explore the grand rooms filled with fine art and antique furniture. The expansive gardens, including fountains, statues, and lakes, are great for a stroll. Don't miss the chance to visit the farm shop and café for some local products.

Goathland

Known to many as the setting for the TV series "Heartbeat" and the Harry Potter films, Goathland is a picturesque village worth viewing. Ride the historical steam train on the North Yorkshire Moors Railway, and take in the beautiful moorland scenery. A visit to the village shops and the local pub will give you a feel of the area's charm.

York

A bit farther away but worth the trip, York is a city steeped in history. Visit the majestic York Minster, walk along the old city walls, and explore the Shambles, a historic street with overhanging timber-framed buildings. The Jorvik Viking Center and the National Railway Museum are also must-see sites.

Scarborough

Scarborough, a lively seaside town, offers a mix of historic places and modern attractions. Explore Scarborough Castle, perched on a headland with sweeping views of the coast. The town also has beautiful parks, museums, and a busy harbor. Scarborough is perfect for a family-friendly day out, with plenty of shops, restaurants, and entertainment choices.

Helmsley

This lovely market town has much to offer. Visit the ruins of Helmsley Castle, and walk through the beautiful Helmsley Walled Garden. The town center is filled with local shops and cafés, making it a delightful place to spend a leisurely day. The nearby National Center for Birds of Prey is also an interesting stop.

Danby

In the heart of the North York Moors National Park, Danby is home to the Moors National Park Center. Learn about the natural and cultural history of the moors through interactive exhibits and enjoy the scenic walking trails. The village itself is lovely, with traditional stone cottages and a welcoming vibe.

Pickering

Pickering is known for its ancient castle and the North Yorkshire Moors Railway. The castle, with its well-preserved keep and towers, offers insight into medieval life. A ride on the heritage steam train from Pickering to Whitby or Grosmont is a highlight of any stay.

SCENIC TRAIN RIDES

North Yorkshire Moors Railway

One of the most famous routes is the North Yorkshire Moors Railway. This heritage railway goes from Whitby to Pickering, passing through the heart of the North York Moors National Park. The journey takes you through dense forests, rolling moorlands, and quaint towns. Along the way, you can stop at stations like Goathland, which acts as the fictional Hogsmeade station from the Harry Potter films. The vintage steam and diesel trains add to the nostalgic experience, making it a unique day out.

Esk Valley Line

Another excellent choice is the Esk Valley Line, which travels from Whitby to Middlesbrough. This path offers a blend of coastal and rural scenery, with views of the North Sea and the beautiful Esk Valley. The train meanders through charming villages such as Grosmont and Glaisdale, giving opportunities to explore these delightful spots. The journey is especially beautiful in the spring and autumn when the fields are vibrant with seasonal colors.

Scarborough Spa Express

For a touch of luxury, try the Scarborough Spa Express. This special excursion runs from York to Scarborough, passing through Whitby at selected times. The route offers great views of the Yorkshire countryside and coastline. The historic train, often hauled by a steam locomotive, offers a grand and relaxing way to travel. Passengers can enjoy a meal on board, making the experience even more pleasant.

Whitby to Robin Hood's Bay

A shorter yet equally delightful trip is the path from Whitby to Robin Hood's Bay. Although not a traditional train ride, this trip on the steam-powered Whitby & Robin Hood's Bay Railway offers a scenic adventure. The ride includes sweeping views of the coast and the North York Moors. Robin Hood's Bay itself is a lovely destination with its historic streets and coastal charm, great for a day trip.

Coastal Rail Trail

For those who enjoy combining train travel with a bit of walking, the Coastal Rail Trail is great. Start your trip by taking the train from Whitby to Scarborough, then follow the coastal path back. This walk offers stunning sea views and a chance to experience the natural beauty of the Yorkshire coast up close. It's a great way to spend a day exploring both by train and on foot.

CHAPTER 10

PRACTICAL INFORMATION

TRANSPORTATION AND GETTING AROUND

Arriving by Car

Driving to Whitby is a popular choice for many tourists. The town is well-connected by road, with the A171 and A169 allowing easy access from major cities like York, Middlesbrough, and Scarborough. Once in Whitby, you'll find several parking choices, including short-stay and long-stay car parks. Popular spots include the Endeavour Wharf Car Park and the Pavilion Top Car Park. It's wise to check for parking fees and availability, especially during peak tourist seasons.

Traveling by Train

Whitby is accessible by train, giving a scenic journey through the North Yorkshire Moors. The Whitby Railway Station, situated close to the town center, connects travelers to the mainline services via Middlesbrough. Northern Rail runs regular services to and from Whitby, making it easy to plan your visit. The train ride itself is an enjoyable experience, offering beautiful views of the countryside.

Using Buses

For those who prefer bus travel, Whitby is well-served by local and regional bus routes. Arriva North East runs routes that connect Whitby to nearby towns and cities. The Coastliner service is highly popular, providing a direct link from Leeds and York to Whitby. The bus station is conveniently located near the town center, making it easy to transfer to local services or continue your trip on foot.

Exploring on Foot

Whitby's small size makes walking one of the best ways to explore the town. Many of the key sites, such as the Whitby Abbey, the Captain Cook Memorial Museum, and the historic harbor, are within walking distance of each other. The town's narrow streets and alleys are filled with unique shops, cafes, and historic buildings, offering plenty of opportunities to find hidden gems along the way.

Taxi and Ride-Sharing Services

Taxis are easily available in Whitby for those who prefer a more private mode of transport. Local taxi companies operate throughout the town and can be booked in advance or hailed on the street. Ride-sharing services are less common but may be available through apps like Uber, based on the time of year and demand.

Cycling in Whitby

For cycling enthusiasts, Whitby offers several bike-friendly paths. The Cinder Track, a disused railway line, provides a scenic bicycle path from Whitby to Scarborough. Bicycles can be rented from local shops, and there are secure bike racks throughout the town for easy parking.

Boat Trips and Ferries

Whitby's coastal setting also means you can explore the area by water. Boat trips and ferries are available from the harbor, giving a unique view of the coastline and the chance to spot marine wildlife. These excursions can be a relaxing way to see the sights and learn more about Whitby's maritime history.

Tips for Getting Around

1. When planning your visit to Whitby, consider the following tips to make your journey smoother:

2. Check the local weather forecast and dress properly for walking or cycling.

3. Pick up a map from the tourist information center to help navigate the town's streets and sites.

4. If you're using public transport, check schedules and plan your trips to avoid any delays.

HEALTH AND SAFETY TIPS

First, make sure you are weather-ready. Because of its seaside location, Whitby experiences rapid weather changes. Pack layers for warmth in the winter and a raincoat for unexpected downpours. You must wear comfortable shoes, particularly if you intend to stroll or hike the picturesque routes in the area. Before leaving, always check the weather forecast and make any necessary adjustments to your plans.

Keep an eye out and be mindful of your surroundings when strolling around Whitby's picturesque streets and historical landmarks. The town may become congested, particularly during the busiest travel seasons. Don't carry a lot of cash, and keep your possessions safe. Pickpockets might be discouraged by carrying a backpack or crossbody bag with tight zippers. Make sure the kids know what to do if they become separated from the group if you are traveling with them.

Whitby's breathtaking beaches and coastline are popular destinations, however, they should be used with prudence. Keep an eye on the tide schedule because the water might swiftly rise and possibly obstruct your path. Remain in the approved swimming areas, heed any posted cautions, and obey lifeguard directions. It is advisable to swim cautiously and never by yourself because the waters can be chilly and occasionally choppy. Wear strong shoes and take caution when walking near cliffs and rock formations as they can be slippery, especially after rain.

Whitby has a wide range of delectable options for people who appreciate trying out local cuisine. Select eateries and food vendors who seem hygienic and well-maintained to prevent any health hazards. Whitby is known for its seafood, but be sure it's fresh and cooked to perfection. To make sure your food is safe, let your server know if you have any dietary restrictions or allergies.

Carry a map or GPS device and stay on designated trails if you intend to hike or explore the countryside. Particularly if you're heading to a remote location, let someone know your itinerary and anticipated time of return. To stay hydrated and focused, pack snacks and drinks. Having a basic first aid kit on hand is also a smart idea in case of small accidents or emergencies.

Whitby's health services are dependable, but in case of an emergency, it's a good idea to know where the closest clinic or hospital is located. Wear a medical alert bracelet if you have a medical condition, and carry any necessary medications with you at all times. Having health emergency coverage on your travel insurance will give you even more peace of mind.

ACCESSIBILITY INFORMATION

Getting Around Whitby

The town is quite hilly, which can present some problems for those with mobility issues. However, there are several ways to travel the area comfortably. Whitby's public transportation includes accessible buses and a railway station with facilities for disabled passengers. Taxis equipped for wheelchair users are also available and can be pre-booked for ease.

Accessible Attractions

Whitby Abbey, one of the town's most famous landmarks, has made major strides in accessibility. There is a visitor center with accessible restrooms, and the grounds have pathways ideal for wheelchairs. A shuttle service is available to help visitors with mobility issues in reaching the abbey from the parking area.

The Captain Cook Memorial Museum, another popular attraction, is housed in a historic building with steps at the entrance. However, the museum offers virtual tours and thorough guides to ensure that all visitors can enjoy learning about Captain Cook's adventures. Additionally, staff members are trained to help visitors with specific needs.

Accommodations

Several hotels and guesthouses in Whitby are equipped with accessible rooms. These places typically offer features such as step-free entrances, ground-floor rooms, wide doorways, and adapted bathrooms. When booking, it is recommended to contact the property directly to confirm the specific accessibility features they provide.

Dining Options

Whitby boasts a variety of restaurants and cafes, many of which are accessible to tourists with disabilities. Numerous establishments have step-free entry and accessible restrooms. For those with dietary restrictions, many restaurants offer gluten-free, vegetarian, and vegan choices, ensuring that everyone can enjoy a meal out.

Parking and Facilities

Whitby has several designated parking spaces for Blue Badge holders, located easily near major attractions and the town center. Public restrooms with disabled facilities are available throughout the town, including at key spots such as the harbor, the abbey, and the main shopping areas.

Support Services

Local groups in Whitby provide support services for visitors with disabilities. These include mobility equipment hire, such as wheelchairs and scooters, which can be planned to ensure availability. The Tourist Information Center can offer advice and assistance on accessibility, including maps and guides showing accessible routes and facilities.

LOCAL ETIQUETTE AND CUSTOMS

One major part of social etiquette in Whitby is courtesy. The people respect good manners, so saying "please" and "thank you" is necessary. A warm welcome like "hello" or "good morning" can go a long way in making a great impression. When visiting businesses or restaurants, it's normal to meet the workers and engage in polite conversation.

Respecting personal space is also vital. The residents of Whitby, like many in the UK, appreciate their personal space, so avoid standing too near to others, especially in queues or on public transportation.

When dining out, it's courteous to wait until everyone at the table is served before starting your meal. Tipping at restaurants is typical, with 10-15% of the bill being a standard gratuity. In pubs, it's normal to take turns paying for rounds of drinks if you are with a group. If someone gives you a drink, it's courteous to reciprocate.

Whitby has a rich marine tradition, and fishing is a vital aspect of the local culture. When visiting the harbor or interacting with fisherman, showing respect for their profession and way of life is welcomed. Avoid interrupting their work or taking images without authorization.

The town also has a significant relationship with literature and history, being the basis for Bram Stoker's "Dracula." When visiting historic locations like Whitby Abbey, it's crucial to show respect for these cultural relics. Follow any guidelines offered, such as keeping on specified walkways and not touching artifacts.

CHAPTER 11

SUSTAINABLE TRAVEL

ECO-FRIENDLY ACCOMMODATION

1. The Woods Eco Lodge

Location: The Woods, Whitby, North Yorkshire, YO21 1BJ

Price: $120-$180 per night

Phone Number: +44 1947 602674

The Woods Eco Lodge is an ideal choice for nature lovers. This lodge emphasizes sustainable practices, such as solar panels, rainwater harvesting, and eco-friendly toiletries. Located near the North York Moors, it provides a serene environment for relaxation and exploration. Guests can enjoy hiking trails, wildlife spotting, and local organic produce.

2. Green Gables Guest House

Location: 17 Crescent Avenue, Whitby, North Yorkshire, YO21 3ED

Price: $90-$140 per night

Phone Number: +44 1947 600471

Green Gables Guest House offers a charming and eco-conscious experience. This Victorian house has been retrofitted with energy-efficient systems and uses locally sourced materials. Guests can enjoy hearty breakfasts made with organic ingredients and relax in the garden that supports local wildlife.

3. The Shepherd's Purse

Location: 95 Church Street, Whitby, North Yorkshire, YO22 4BH

Price: $100-$150 per night

Phone Number: +44 1947 820774

The Shepherd's Purse is a unique, family-run accommodation that focuses on sustainability. It features cozy rooms with recycled and upcycled furnishings. This guest house supports local artisans and provides eco-friendly toiletries. Its central location makes it easy to explore Whitby's historic sites and the nearby coastline.

4. La Rosa Hotel

Location: 5 East Terrace, Whitby, North Yorkshire, YO21 3HB

Price: $130-$200 per night

Phone Number: +44 1947 606981

La Rosa Hotel offers a blend of vintage charm and modern sustainability. The hotel employs green practices such as energy-efficient lighting, organic linens, and biodegradable cleaning products. Guests can appreciate themed rooms and stunning views of Whitby Abbey, making their stay both memorable and environmentally responsible.

5. YHA Whitby

Location: Abbey House, East Cliff, Whitby, North Yorkshire, YO22 4JT

Price: $30-$70 per night

Phone Number: +44 345 371 9524

YHA Whitby is perfect for budget-conscious travelers looking for eco-friendly accommodations. This hostel, set in a historic building, incorporates various green initiatives, including waste reduction programs and sustainable energy use. It offers shared and private rooms, a communal kitchen, and stunning views of the North Sea.

GREEN ACTIVITIES AND TOURS

Visit the North York Moors National Park to begin your journey. Hiking, cycling, and animal viewing abound on this expansive stretch of heather moorland, woodlands, and shoreline. The park offers a variety of routes that are appropriate for hikers of all experience levels, as well as breathtaking scenery, clean air, and the opportunity to encounter local species. There are accessible guided tours that provide an understanding of the distinct history and ecology of the area.

Consider taking a walk along the Cleveland Way National Trail along the shore for a more immersive experience. This long-distance path passes through Whitby and provides access to gorgeous beaches and cliffs as well as amazing vistas of the sea. Along with being a fantastic workout, walking this trail offers the opportunity to take in the striking coastline and its geological characteristics. Remember to stop by Saltwick Bay, a well-liked location for fossil exploration.

Another fantastic way to take in the natural beauty of the area is to take one of Whitby's boat trips. Many companies provide environmentally conscious boat cruises that give a distinctive viewpoint of the coast while reducing their negative effects on the ecosystem. These tours are fascinating and instructive for people of all ages since they frequently offer the chance to see marine life, including seals, dolphins, and different seabirds.

A must-visit for anyone interested in flora is the Whitby Community Garden. In addition to encouraging sustainable growing methods, this town's volunteer-run garden offers a tranquil haven. Organic farming, composting, and the value of biodiversity are among the topics covered for visitors. The garden also holds entertaining and educational courses and events.

There are many routes for cyclists to explore in and around Whitby. An old railroad track called the Cinder Track is a well-liked option.

This 21-mile track offers a picturesque ride across the countryside and connects Whitby and Scarborough. There are many places to pause and enjoy the scenery, making it an excellent way to explore the terrain at your speed.

Birdwatching at Whitby Abbey Headland is another interesting activity. This historic site is a great place to see a variety of bird species in addition to providing a window into the past. Many seabirds can be seen on the cliffs and nearby areas, and the expansive vistas make for a lovely setting for a leisurely day of birdwatching.

Consider going on a guided eco-tour for a distinctive and environmentally friendly experience. The main goals of these trips are to inform visitors about the local fauna, conservation initiatives, and the value of preserving natural environments. These tours are given by knowledgeable guides who offer a deeper understanding of the environmental significance of the area.

Finally, one satisfying method to help preserve Whitby's shoreline is to take part in beach cleanups. Regular cleanups are arranged by a variety of community organizations and volunteer groups, allowing locals and guests to contribute to the upkeep of the beaches' cleanliness and wildlife safety.

SUPPORTING LOCAL BUSINESSES

Supporting local businesses in Whitby is not just a good deed; it's a way to experience the town's true essence. By choosing to shop, dine, and stay at local establishments, you contribute to the community's economic growth and preserve its unique charm and character.

One of the most rewarding ways to support Whitby's local businesses is by shopping at its independent stores. These shops offer a variety of unique products that reflect the town's culture and creativity. From handmade crafts and artisanal goods to fresh local produce, the items you find here are often one-of-a-kind and crafted with care. By purchasing from these stores, you help sustain local artisans and producers, ensuring they can continue their trades and pass on their skills to future generations.

Dining at local restaurants and cafes is another excellent way to support Whitby's economy. These establishments often source their ingredients from nearby farms and producers, offering you a taste of the region's freshest and finest. Whether you're enjoying a hearty breakfast, a light lunch, or a sumptuous dinner, you can savor the flavors that are distinct to Whitby. Moreover, by eating locally, you help reduce the carbon footprint associated with food transportation, contributing to a more sustainable environment.

Staying at locally-owned accommodations, such as bed and breakfasts, boutique hotels, and guesthouses, provides a more personal and memorable experience. These places often have a story to tell and offer a warm, welcoming atmosphere that large chain hotels cannot match. The owners take pride in their hospitality and are usually more than happy to share their knowledge of the area, suggesting hidden gems and lesser-known attractions that you might otherwise miss.

Participating in local events and festivals is also a wonderful way to support the community. These events often showcase the talents of local artists, musicians, and performers, providing them with a platform to reach a wider audience. By attending these events, you not only enjoy a fun and engaging experience but also help promote and sustain Whitby's cultural heritage.

Supporting local businesses in Whitby also means advocating for them. Word of mouth is a powerful tool; by recommending your favorite local spots to friends and family, you help spread the word and bring more business to the area. Sharing your positive experiences on social media and leaving favorable reviews online can also make a significant impact, attracting more visitors and encouraging them to support local enterprises.

TIPS FOR REDUCING YOUR CARBON FOOTPRINT

In Whitby, lowering your carbon footprint can have a positive and fulfilling effect. There are several eco-friendly living options available in this quaint seaside town, and your actions can contribute to maintaining its natural beauty for future generations.

First, think about your means of transportation. Since Whitby is a walking town, try to avoid driving and instead explore on foot. You'll not only cut emissions but also find undiscovered treasures as you go. Rent a bicycle or take public transit for longer trips. The local bus service is a convenient alternative because it is dependable and serves most regions.

When it comes to accommodations, pick environmentally friendly options. In Whitby, there are a lot of lodging establishments that are dedicated to eco-friendly methods. Seek out locations that recycle, use renewable energy, and reduce waste. Remaining in such locations helps environmentally conscious enterprises.

Another practical strategy to reduce your carbon footprint is to eat locally. Whitby is home to a wide range of eateries and cafés that purchase their food from nearby fishermen and farms. Consuming locally grown products lowers emissions by reducing the need for long-distance transportation. In addition, the food tastes better and is typically fresher.

Carrying reusable products will help you reduce waste. To prevent using single-use plastics, carry a water bottle, shopping bag, and coffee cup with you. In Whitby, a lot of stores and cafes would gladly fill your reusable containers. Making this simple adjustment can cut down on the quantity of plastic garbage you produce considerably.

Encourage regional conservation initiatives. Whitby is home to several environmental preservation-focused organizations. Contributions or time volunteering for these organizations can have a significant impact. Take part in wildlife conservation initiatives, beach clean-ups, or educational events to contribute to the preservation of the region's distinctive ecosystems.

It's also critical to conserve energy. Whether you're renting a place or staying in a hotel, pay attention to how much energy you consume. To save energy, turn off the lights, disconnect electronics when not in use, and adjust the thermostat. Energy consumption can be significantly reduced by taking these small steps.

Another way to help is to shop sustainably. Whitby offers a variety of stores that sell handcrafted items and environmentally friendly products. Select products that are manufactured from sustainable materials, come in minimal packaging, or help out local craftspeople. Making well-considered purchases can help the community's economy and lessen waste.

Lastly, convey to others the significance of lowering their carbon impact. Tell your friends and family about your experiences and advice. When they travel to Whitby or any other location, urge them to make environmentally friendly decisions. We can change a lot when we work together since group effort is very effective.

CONCLUSION

As we reach the end of our journey through the charming town of Whitby, we hope you feel as enchanted by its cobbled streets, haunting history, and stunning seaside views as we are. From the dramatic ruins of Whitby Abbey, standing proudly atop the East Cliff, to the warm and welcoming atmosphere of the local pubs and eateries, Whitby offers a blend of adventure and tranquility that caters to every traveler's desires.

Throughout this guide, we've explored not only the iconic landmarks like the 199 Steps and the Whitby Museum but also hidden gems that give Whitby its unique character. Whether it was the thrill of ghost walks, the discovery of maritime heritage, or the serenity of sandy beaches, each experience was curated to enhance your visit, ensuring memories that will last a lifetime.

For those who relish culinary delights, we introduce you to Whitby's famous fish and chips and the irresistible charm of its tearooms and cafes. Adventurers were guided through scenic trails and heritage tours, while culture enthusiasts delved into the rich tapestry of music festivals and art galleries.

As you close this guide, remember that Whitby isn't just a place to visit; it's a destination to experience, live, and love. Whether you're seeking a peaceful retreat or an exciting exploration, Whitby awaits you with open arms and endless possibilities.

Don't let this book be the end of your journey. Make Whitby your next travel destination and immerse yourself in its enchanting allure. Book your trip, pack your bags, and set sail for an unforgettable adventure in the heart of North Yorkshire. Whitby is calling are you ready to answer?

Printed in Great Britain
by Amazon